SMALL PATIOS

Simple Projects, Contemporary Designs

A GARDEN DESIGN BOOK

SMALL PATIOS

Simple Projects, Contemporary Designs

HAZEL WHITE

Photography by Saxon Holt

CHRONICLE BOOKS
SAN FRANCISCO

Dedicated to:

My sweet mother, Hilda White (HW)

The gardener in me, my father (SH)

Library of Congress
Cataloging-in-Publication Data:
White, Hazel.
Small patios: simple projects, contemporary
designs / by Hazel White; photography by
Saxon Holt.
p.   cm.
Includes bibliographical references and index.
ISBN 0-8118-2542-6 (pbk.)
1. Patios. I. Title.
TH4970.W46 2001
690'.893—dc21   00-024126

Printed in Hong Kong

Designed and typeset by David Bullen Design

Distributed in Canada by Raincoast Books
9050 Shaughnessy Street
Vancouver, British Columbia V6P 6E5

10 9 8 7 6 5 4 3 2 1

Chronicle Books LLC
85 Second Street
San Francisco, California 94105

www.chroniclebooks.com

CONTENTS

INTRODUCTION

A garden patio invites you to leave the house and live outdoors. Add a chair and a place to put up your feet, and you can read the headlines of the morning newspaper in the fresh air while you also read the clouds and the prospect of warmth or rain. Later in the day, you might bring refreshments outside for friends, and all stay to watch the moon rise through the garden trees.

The desire to live outdoors grows as our homes and cities become crowded and work takes place more and more indoors. But the desire is fickle. We leave the comfort of the house only perhaps if we see sunlight playing over the seat of an outdoor chair and a trumpet vine's flowers blowing soft and rosy pink in the air. A patio needs a special quality. To set our feet in motion, it must be convivial like an indoor room and yet also be open to the flowers, trees, and sky. Then we are drawn irresistibly by the adventure of finding a sheltered place in the wild, a tug so strong that it's probably written in our bones.

In visiting gardens for this book, I saw a kaleidoscope of beautiful outdoor living spaces. Some patios offered an exhilarating view, others an intimate refuge in the heart of a city. Some were true extensions of the indoor living room, the flooring continued straight over the threshold into the garden and out toward the trees, the furniture as elegant and comfortable as indoors. In other gardens, tiny patios—no more than stopping places—had been created to catch a pleasant view over a fence or to take advantage of a sheltered spot out of the wind.

A large outdoor patio close to the house is a luxury, like a large living room and dining room indoors. With such a patio, you can hold birthday parties outdoors and invite lots of neighbors to drop by for an afternoon in the sun. More essential than this kind of patio, however, are the small resting places you might distribute through the garden, hideaways from which to admire the winter light on a bank of ornamental grasses or to get as far away from the domestic sounds of the house as you can. These mini-patios, in which you can make a floor as informal as you please, are precious invitations to spend more time outdoors.

The English farmhouse I grew up in had no planned spaces, large or small, for outdoor living. Beneath the tall walls and crab apple trees that ringed the garden, lines of vegetables and rectangles of lawn ran right up to the dahlias, wallflowers, and roses at the house. The weather was too cool for sitting outdoors most of the year, and in the summer we were usually working in the fields. There we ate our lunch and tea sandwiches out of biscuit tins, sitting on a floor of prickly straw stubble with our backs against the day's new bales. In the fifteen minutes after eating before returning to work, we lay on top of the bales for the breeze or in the shelter provided by a tractor wheel or a hawthorn hedge. On misty mornings before the dew dried on the machinery, we waited for the other workers on the rise in the field where the sun would first scale the hedgerows and warm our cold faces.

Now a longtime city dweller in a much warmer climate, I still search for the perfect place to catch a bit of sun, a sense of shelter, and a whisper of breeze. I've put a table and chairs on the patio next to the kitchen for a view of the sky and a glimpse of the San Francisco Bay (the house is small, so I poach the garden furniture if several friends come to dinner). Sometimes I leave the warm house wall and sit in the sun trap on the garden steps where I can watch the minute goings-on in a thicket of purple hopseed bush and gaze out to a trio of bowling balls under the plum tree.

Some balmy night, I'm going to extend the use of the decomposed granite patio I built a few years ago at the end of the garden. It is thick now with the seeds of the overhanging birch trees; wild mushrooms grow there in the shade, and a stone "sleeping head" rests in a small clearing. I'm dreaming of camping there, on the cushioned bench under the hood of the trees, and cooking breakfast when the sun rises.

Each patio in this book shows how its owner wanted to live outdoors. There are rooms designed for sophisticated outdoor dining, cozy sitting places, smart entrance patios separated from the street, and many garden alcoves and hideaways built to offer a place of peace.

If you're starting a new patio or remodeling an old one, look through the first chapter, "Designing Patios." Patios are attractive and used frequently only if they are partially enclosed and yet open to some kind of view. The chapter contains many such secrets of successful patio design. The next chapter, "Building Patios," describes the practical business of patio construction: tools to buy and rent, suggestions for clearing weeds and testing drainage, and many tips about setting the work up right.

The patio "recipes," in the chapters that follow, include all the information you need: lists of tools, materials, and plants, and the how-to steps for creating each patio. The patios are all relatively easy to build. Those categorized as moderately difficult merely contain more steps than the others, or require more attention to detail or a certain level of confidence using a cutting tool, for example. If you've never handled a brick or a trowel, take the stress out of the project by determining from the beginning to work slowly and, if you like, accepting any help offered by friends.

Building a patio is a process of discovery. As you build, you'll learn a great many particulars about the site—the color and texture of the soil, the lay of the land in this part of your garden, the patterns of the sunlight at different times of day, the temperature changes, and the fragrances wafting in the air. When the patio is done, you'll have a special attachment to this particular piece of the earth and know exactly where you want to place a chair.

DESIGNING PATIOS

Patios connect us to the wild: to the breeze scented with heat or moisture blowing in off the hills, to the cycles of sunlight and darkness, and to our memories of the outdoors. They also connect us to our gardens. Lured first by the chance to read or sleep in the sun on the patio, we start to daydream and putter—and may end up canceling errands and spending the rest of the morning weeding or lost in reverie. This chapter contains the secrets of designing a patio that pulls people outdoors.

PATIOS CONNECTED TO THE HOUSE ◐◑ In the most beautiful living spaces, the indoors merges almost imperceptibly with the outdoors. The floor, whether it's made of bamboo or marble tile, runs uninterrupted over the threshold and the two spaces to either side of it provide shelter, comfort, and patterns of natural light. In the balmy seasons, you can cross in and out without thinking, without considering whether to put on shoes or take everything you might need with you. True extensions of the indoor living space, patios connected to the house are the most frequently used patios of all.

To establish a sense of continuity over the threshold, consider using the same floor material outdoors and indoors if that's feasible; if it's not, choose materials similar in texture and color. Carry the colors of the indoor room over into the outdoors—for example, into the bench cushions or the outdoor table linen—and coordinate the style and material of the furniture in both areas. Consider too what kinds of plants might thrive in both places.

Because a patio connected to the house lures people gradually into the outdoors, it makes a comfortable transition into the garden proper. With that ambiguous place between the two, even on a cool day you can be lured out along a path by the light on the lawn and the smell of the grass; without it, the garden may stay unused, no matter how beautiful it is once you're there. So be sure to link the patio to the garden with an attractive path and tempt people to walk it by providing a glimpse of the next destination.

A patio connected to the house is also immensely practical. A cool drink or an extra chair is always at hand.

REMOTE PATIOS ✐◞ What a patio away from the house loses in terms of convenience, it gains in terms of surprise. A remote patio can be an adventure into the outdoors. There's often a frisson of excitement about eating or sleeping there, hidden under a tree or at the edge of a view.

The destination of the main garden path is a natural place for a patio away from the house; practically, it provides space for people to turn around before resuming the path back to the house, but more importantly it provides a sense of having arrived somewhere worth the journey out.

Other natural places for remote patios include stopping places along the path. Make one wherever you want people to pause and admire a flower bed or the best view of the house or to enjoy a spot that's in the sun and out of the wind. To make the patio feel comfortable, build it off to one side of the path, like a turnout, rather than running the path through the middle of it. I use the term patio but in a natural garden, you might scratch a clearing out of the dirt or let the stepping-stone path swell into a pool of stones so there's space for two or three people to stand together and talk.

The place in the garden that you love the most—for any reason, even an inexplicable one—should have at least a space for a chair. Famous California landscape architect Thomas Church recommended that you walk around the house a few times. "In some places you will walk fast, but sooner or later you will reach a spot where you feel in repose. It may be the lines of the house or the position of the trees, or you may never know why; but it could be the place for your terrace." Chances are other people will love that place too. You might eventually turn it into a proper garden destination with a floor and a sense of scale that suits its special character.

ONE PATIO OR A DOZEN? ✐◞ In Santa Barbara, California, there's a modest house among native oaks high on a hillside with a half-dozen outdoor rooms with patio floors. From the living room, stone tiles go across the threshold between sliding glass doors onto a long veranda along the back of the house. Here an outdoor living room—rattan sofa, cushioned armchairs, coffee table, rug, sun blinds—faces the view through the oaks over the valley. An office off one end of the veranda has its own paved square in front of it, with an unplanted arbor casting bars of shadow on the floor. An outdoor room with low walls, lawn, and a central fountain adjoins the outdoor living room. A dining patio is situated below the veranda at the house corner, under the oaks. Around the corner, the stone gives way to more informal spaces: a bedroom opens onto a patio where strips of mondo grass grow between square pavers; from there a path leads beyond the house to the edge of the hillside and another patio with a sunrise view.

Like rooms indoors, some of the outdoor rooms are public, some private. Some open onto one another to accommodate a crowd and allow people to move freely and comfortably into the sun or back into dappled or full shade. Farthest from the living room are the places designed for contemplation and quietness.

In a small garden, it's just as important that there be a range of spaces. The options are to build one large patio, either a central courtyard or a patio that wraps around the house walls, with quiet areas or alcoves built into it; or to make two or three small patios along or off the main path. In the latter case, try to keep a long view open through the patios, to create a sense of spaciousness.

Almost always a garden has at least one overlooked opportunity for an extra patio. Consider widening a path or the surround to a pool or a pond. Build generous landings into flights of outdoor stairs. Perhaps a slope could be pushed back behind a retaining wall to make a pleasant outdoor extension to the kitchen, or screens could be placed in a side yard to make an outdoor room beside a bedroom there. The garden boundary sometimes has possibilities; it's often sunnier and quieter than the areas close to the house, and a rose arch might be all that's necessary to ensure enough privacy. A tool shed or workshop might have a small entrance patio with a simple seat. As you would if you were designing indoor space, consider who uses each area, and try to give each person in the household a personal place.

PATIO SIZE ✑ It's a common mistake to make a patio too small. Because the patio sits in the outdoors, to feel right it needs to be larger than an equivalent indoor space. How large to make it depends on the scale of the house, the scale of the surroundings, and also of course how you plan to use the space. Always it's better to err on the side of large.

Take into account the size of your outdoor furniture, usually heftier than indoor furniture, and the space you must leave around each piece for people to walk by or to settle themselves in—for an outdoor dining table that's at least 5 feet all around the table edge. Just as in decorating an indoor room, it's best not to push the furniture right up against the walls; a space of 9 inches between the wall and the back of the bench makes a gracious detail. Don't forget to factor in the space for plant containers, side tables, extra chairs, storage units for cushions, and the rather large amount of space some plants need. A simple 4-foot bench needs a space 6 feet long (1 foot free on either end) and 6 feet deep to allow for foot room and space for someone to walk by. We usually drastically underestimate how large a patio needs to be to feel comfortable. If it has ample space, you can be sure that during construction it'll look huge.

Although tiny patios seem feasible for use by one person, it's advisable to make a patio at least 5 or 6 feet deep. A space smaller than that is uninviting.

SUN OR SHADE? ✑ People who spend a lot of time indoors like to be able to walk out on the weekends into the sun. Even on a warm, bright day, a table in the sun under an umbrella is more appealing than a place in full shade. Where there's little light, the atmosphere is usually gloomy and not conducive to outdoor living.

The presence of sunlight is perhaps the most important factor in how much a patio is used. Others are the absence of wind and the convenience of the location, how close it is to the house. Because sunlight is so important, avoid the north-facing side of the house for a patio; it will be in perpetual shade from the house. Except in the hottest climates, a south-facing site is best, because it will receive sunshine all day (unless there are towering trees or buildings nearby). A west-facing patio is useful for entertaining late in the day (in some climates, you'll need umbrellas and sunglasses) and for catching sunsets. An east-facing patio may lose the sun before lunch is over.

The pattern of the sun, of course, changes from season to season. In summer the sun travels directly overhead through the middle of the day; in winter it makes an arc lower in the sky. The length of shadows from buildings changes according to the position of the sun; they are short when the sun is overhead, long when the sun is low in the sky. If you are surrounded by buildings or trees, you'll probably know only after living in a house for a year where the sunshine and shadows fall.

If your yard is on the north side of your house, consider building the patio away from the house, out of its shadow. To make sure the patio is used, perhaps build an arm to the patio that connects it to the house. Alternatively, build a wraparound patio that takes you around the house corner into the sunlight on the west or east side. Or enclose the house entrance, on the south side, to make a private space there. If you already have a shady patio, you may have noticed that you'd rather drink your coffee on the front steps in the sun.

Having said all that, the perfect patio offers sunshine and shade. The sunshine should pool at the house, so you cross from the indoors out into light. The shade might be at the far reach of the patio, where it meets a tree. There is something marvelously soothing about watching the shadows of tree branches flicker over a floor, the motion and pattern changing with the breeze. And the contrast between light and shade in a garden is sensuous and dramatic. If there's a chance of having both on your main patio, don't miss it.

In a small garden, choose a patio tree carefully. Look for an open tree with delicate leaves, such as a Japanese maple *(Acer palmatum)* or silk tree *(Albizia julibrissin),* which will let sunlight through the foliage. Above all else, make sure it's the right size to let your patio keep its precious portion of sunshine. If there's little space for shade, consider a vine-covered arbor at the patio edge, or an awning or umbrella. On a patio just 6 feet deep designed by landscape architect Isabelle Greene, a wisteria vine pruned up into a tree and placed in a pot on a base with wheels allows the shade to be wheeled around the space according to the position of the sun.

REFUGE FROM WIND, RAIN, AND COLD ◠◡ To be habitable, a patio needs to be sheltered from prevailing steady winds. A breeze may be welcome, especially in a hot-summer climate, but wind will clear the patio of people as quickly as rain. Before you start to build, be sure you understand the wind patterns in your garden. It isn't enough to know the direction of prevailing winds; wind barriers near the patio site, such as buildings and neighbors' trees and fences, can alter the wind patterns significantly. For example, an impermeable barrier such as a house or solid wood fence will cause wind turbulence on the leeward side; the wind will roll down over the house or fence onto the patio like a waterfall. Although shelter can be built with trees and tall shrubs or permeable fences, it's easier to choose a naturally sheltered site.

Being outdoors during a rainstorm can be an exhilarating experience, so, rather than making people run to the house for cover or closing down the patio during changeable weather, consider giving part of the patio a ceiling. It might be an awning, a simple tin roof or roof overhang, or a thickly planted arbor. Alternatively, place the entire patio within a gazebo, settling it into the site with shrubs and vines on three sides, so it doesn't look like an off-the-shelf bandstand.

An outdoor fireplace is luxurious. It assures the greatest comfort and sets the mind dreaming of sparks and firelight under a night sky. You can have a regular fireplace built into an outdoor wall or much more simply buy a couple of fired-clay chimineas or braziers to move around the patio floor.

ENCLOSURE ⁊⧀ Studies of how people use public open space (described in *A Pattern Language,* by Christopher Alexander and his colleagues) have shown that most of us prefer to sit with our backs against something, in a relatively protected space with a view. To make your patio a naturally comfortable space, partially enclose it. The ideal site is in the corner formed by an L-shaped house; the patio is then fully enclosed on two sides, which is about the right amount for most people.

Hedges are inexpensive substitutes for walls. So are fences, trellises, and columns. You don't need a tall or a solid barrier; the suggestion of enclosure formed by columns at the patio corners and a low open trellis will do very well. A ceiling is another option for partially enclosing a patio. The simplest is perhaps a series of wires running between posts and covered with vines.

PRIVACY ⁊⧀ A garden that lacks privacy fails as a living space. The garden might be beautifully planted with rare and colorful plants, and the paths might make an enchanting journey through them, but people will settle to read or daydream only if there's an alcove or a rose arch tucked away out of the public view.

Be careful, though, not to overdo the screening around your patio in an attempt to make it perfectly private. It may sound counterintuitive to people who love solitude, but total privacy is undesirable in an outdoor room. Solid tall walls, even green leafy ones, with no path through the space and no views out of it will create a forbidding, isolated atmosphere.

Aim for a happy medium. Plant bamboo to block the view from a neighbor's deck, or build solid walls if you are trying to screen noise, but leave the patio at least half open—so you can't doubt for a moment that you are out in the elements and connected to the larger world. Those are essential qualities of any successful outdoor room.

An indoor room is a poor model when considering how much privacy you need for a patio. Consider instead Vita Sackville-West's rose bower at Sissinghurst Castle in England—a roof of roses growing on a wrought iron frame, with flowers and foliage loosely climbing the posts in the four corners and cascading from the iron ceiling, and every side open to the garden. Or designer Sarah Hammond's wood pile—two adjoining walls of neatly stacked logs, a chair in the corner on a gravel floor, a tin roof overhead, and two sides of the space open to the air and garden views.

VIEWS   We are in awe of those designer houses in magazines with views from the terrace of a sunset over the ocean or a snow-capped mountain range. The truth is that if we lived there or dined there very often, the impact of the view would fade. Recognizing this fact, many designers place a patio so a view enters the space in panels or tantalizing glimpses. If there's no splendid view, they create tantalizing glimpses of other things.

First, walk all through your garden looking for an interesting detail in the view outside it. That might be a neighbor's treetops or a weathervane on someone else's shed or an old brick factory chimney or city lights at night. It need only be the size of a glimpse; you can work out how to screen the rest of the view if it's undesirable. Consider borrowing anything you can from outside your property line to open the view out.

Next, look for views inside the garden. Place your patio to take advantage of the best view of the flower beds or the pond or the pattern of the terraces on the hill. If the patio is away from the house, perhaps there's a pretty view back to the house through a tree. To intensify the view, frame it through branches or a gap in a hedge, or tunnel it between lines of clipped shrubs or lavender. You might also put a literal picture frame around it (see page 53).

A sight that we find interesting but that is often overlooked as an appropriate garden view is a glimpse of people doing things. You might not want the entire neighboring schoolyard as a view, but a cameo of the children on the swings is worth saving. Inside the garden, consider a partial view of the swimming pool or tennis court or vegetable garden.

Finally, consider creating a view. For example, cut a window through a hedge or a shrub border beside the patio and place a birdbath or a fountain beyond it as the view. It is particularly striking if the view out is through a dark wall or hedge and the birdbath is bathed in sunlight. Alternatively, ornament the back gate and make that the view; if the view beyond the gate is worth borrowing, trade a solid gate for a grille.

You can also lead the eye out of the patio by planting a gold- or purple-foliaged tree or shrub at your property line or by grouping a series of brightly planted containers there. A traditional trompe l'oeil painted onto a wall is too kitschy for most people's tastes, but a mirror well placed among vining foliage will trick you for a while into thinking there's a window onto a brightly lit garden there. A suggestion of a view can also sometimes work dramatically: A door or a shuttered window in the garden wall breaks up the enclosure psychologically even when there's nothing behind it. An attractive path leading away through the boundary creates a similar anticipation of a world beyond.

FOCAL POINTS AND PERIMETERS ✿ An indoor room needs a focal point, such as a fireplace, and at least a few interesting details on the walls or around the edges of the room. An outdoor room needs exactly the same treatment: a place where the eye comes naturally to rest, such as a fountain or a table or an arch, and plants or a view or a seat, or all three, at the patio boundaries. A patio arranged this way encourages people to move around it casually and comfortably, to let themselves be led on a whim from reading in the shade to watering the plants and leaning over the patio rail in the sun.

The simplest focal points and boundary details are often the most effective.

Water makes a natural focal point, even still water in a plain bowl if it's set in the sunshine so that it sparkles. And a single fragrant plant or a plant with splotched yellow leaves will draw people across the patio to take a closer look.

DECORATING A PATIO ⌒⌒ Like an indoor room, a patio can quickly become a depository of miscellaneous objects. To prevent that, establish a style for your outdoor living space. Choose one that suits the architecture and the interior design of the house if the patio sits outside the kitchen or living room. Place sculpture or art on the walls as you might indoors, or line the walls with wood or metal shelves and place a collection of succulents or seashells there. A patio away from the house can be decorated in any style—minimally, with a few wildflowers and a boulder from the site, or as a flight of Victorian fancy enveloped by the greenery.

Plain walls and small-textured hedges and vines make excellent backgrounds for decorative objects. Unless you're good at composing rooms with bright wallpaper, colorful carpets and upholstery, and myriad decorative objects, don't be ambitious. Build your outdoor room with natural, unfussy, subdued materials, and ornament it very simply. As landscape architect Thomas Church explains in *Gardens Are for People,* "If the eye sees too many things, it is confused, and the sense of peace is obliterated." Keep in mind that the most enchanting details are the dew on a leaf, the sunlight warming wood, and the trace of pine in the breeze.

PATIO POTS ⌒⌒ Many beautiful pot designs are available and there are umpteen different ways to plant them: all purple foxgloves, white and purple foxgloves, bouquets of foxgloves and ferns, wild grasses and wildflowers, a botanical collection of sedums, a rhododendron, an orange tree, an oak, or maybe simply no plants at all. It's necessary to have a plan; otherwise the clutter and miscellany will irritate your guests.

Landscape architect Russell Page, who built fashionable gardens in Europe in the mid-twentieth century, had strict rules about the subject. For flowers, plain terra-cotta pots, no swags of anything on the pot sides, a single type of flower in each pot, and lots of pots together to make a fine show: "For instance, round a very large pot with a pink oleander," he wrote in the early 1960s, "I would put a whole ring of medium-sized flower pots planted with pink geraniums and, where there was room, I might add still another ring of quite small pots with white or pink petunias." Pots with decorative swags he believed should be used only for orange or lemon trees in predominantly flowerless settings. He loved plain, classy wooden Versailles tubs for magnolias on a house terrace and never used pots with colorful glazes "as their shiny surface seen out of doors makes too brilliant a juxtaposition with flowers or foliage," though they might be used as decorations in themselves, unplanted.

It's advisable to develop a similarly strict aesthetic in patio pots, but yours might run along the lines of matching metallic-looking plants to metal containers or picking up the colors of the pot in the colors of the plants' fall foliage. Keep in mind the power of a simple arrangement, such as a line of lavender along a patio wall all in the same-size terra-cotta pots (for great proportion, the pot height roughly half the height of the flower stems). Simplicity is refreshing—and easy to achieve and maintain.

FURNITURE ⌒⌒ Patio furniture needs to be both beautiful to look at, because it's part of the garden view, and comfortable to sit on. If one quality must take precedence and you want the patio to be used, it must be comfort. Stone is the most durable furniture material but it's the least comfortable garden seating, because it's unyielding and chilly. Wood furniture can be quite comfortable if the backs of the chairs slope a little and the seats are curved, but it is usually bulky and takes considerable space to store. Hardwood (if you can, buy products made from renewable sources) is far more durable than softwood, which needs regular painting or staining. Check with the supplier about the life span of wood pieces if you plan to leave them outside in wet-winter climates. Rattan and wicker are elegant and comfy, but again they are bulky to store and won't last if left out in the rain.

The easiest types of furniture to store are wood-slat French café furniture and canvas directors' chairs. The pieces fold, and they aren't heavy. Some new types of metal furniture are also lightweight, but be sure what you choose won't rust. The best plan is to try out a range of furniture so that you can judge the comfort yourself, and ask the supplier about the required maintenance. One last thing before you buy: check the furniture legs to be sure they won't wobble on your floor.

Benches have a place at the house entrance (mainly as a place for changing shoes and leaving pruners) and as decorative objects at the end of a garden vista. They aren't popular for seating more than one person, because people prefer to sit at an angle to one another rather than side by side. Benches are also relatively heavy and awkward to move.

The most convivial seating is single chairs placed in a rough circle. People will consciously or unconsciously size up the best-looking seat as they approach. Most prefer a seat with its back to a wall, so that it's at least a little sheltered. Chairs that don't match probably have the edge over a matching set, because they offer more choice. If a couple of extra chairs are on hand and all the chairs are easy to move, the seating arrangement will seem particularly flexible and friendly.

In a small space (patio furniture takes up a great deal of room; see page 14) or a space with no storage, consider built-in seating along the patio edge or on the top of a low retaining wall. The seat should be at least 18 inches deep for comfort; make it wider, and you can use it as a serving table too.

For an inexpensive suite of patio furniture, make use of logs, planks, and flat-topped boulders if you have them on site. Throw a pretty fabric over a garage sale table, or carry out some furniture from the living room for the afternoon.

PAVING MATERIALS ✐✐ Paving materials have different characteristics: some are frost-proof, some waterproof; some absorb heat, some reflect it and cause dazzle; some get slippery, either because the surface is so sleek or because they are pocked and collect water and ice. Run through the changes in your climate from season to season, and think about who will be using the patio and what they will be wearing on their feet.

In harsh-winter climates where the ground freezes, terra-cotta and soft brick will crumble, concrete may crack, slate will be slippery, and brick and light-colored (but not white) gravel will look warm. In hot-summer areas, light-colored gravel or stone may be dazzling in the bright sun and too hot.

Choosing a single paving material throughout the garden establishes a pleasant sense of unity; it ties together the various spaces, even if they are decorated differently. Alternatively, be as creative and varied as you please in the patio surfaces, and unify the garden in some other way—for example, with repeated hedges or a repeated plant palette.

Designers usually choose a relatively formal material close to the house and progressively more natural materials as the garden approaches the wild landscape. The patio at the house entrance, for example, might be cut stone and the patio at the end of the garden under the trees, gray gravel colonized by violets. The one golden rule is that the patio material at the house should suit the house architecture.

If you want to draw attention to the boundaries of your patio and differentiate it as a special place, make it of a different material than you use for the paths. Walking from a gravel path over the patio threshold onto cut stone, for example, provides a strong visual and sensory cue that you are entering a different kind of space.

PAVING PATTERNS ☙ Most paving has a natural pattern, which you can sometimes soften or make more dominant by laying it in a certain way. For example, the eye goes to the pattern of the individual stones in a dark flagstone patio if the joints between the stones are filled with white mortar or a light gravel; if you color the mortar to match the stone, the eye goes to the overall shape of the patio instead.

A pattern can be directional. Brick or rectangles of stone laid in courses running across the patio make the patio look wider; if the courses are laid along the length of the patio, it seems longer. Tall or creeping plants on the patio obscure and soften the geometry.

A richly patterned floor might form the main ornament in an outdoor room. Create a complex mosaic of many different materials or settle for a simpler pattern by combining brick with stone or stone with gravel. If you have in mind a quiet patio surface, with no pattern of its own, choose gravel or decomposed granite.

LOW MAINTENANCE BY DESIGN ☙ Cut stone laid edge to edge, on a firm deep base, with a strong edging if necessary and sand packed firmly in the joints, needs only an occasional hosing or sweeping. But be sure the stone isn't prone to staining; some stone is particularly porous and requires regular scrubbing or regular applications of a stone sealant to keep it clean. Gravel needs regular raking and weeding and a light replenishing every year or two. Tightly laid brick needs less weeding than brick spaced widely so that moss and grass can grow in the cracks. Brick or stone patios with mortar in the joints will not need weeding if you check and renew the mortar periodically, but the patio becomes much harder to re-lay if it starts to heave.

In wet or snowy weather, sprinkle sand over stone, brick, and concrete to increase traction and prevent accidents. For safety reasons, keep all patios clear of rotting debris, which can be very slippery.

Low-maintenance patios improve with wear. They were designed so that weather would soften the color and moss would bring a beautiful patina of age. Before you build, gauge the effect of wear on your patio and the need for maintenance. Pay particular attention to any tree litter that will fall or blow there. Consider building a patio that's already invaded by plants, by design; weeds will have a much harder time gaining a toehold there. Above all else, avoid the need to re-lay the surface by building carefully and well.

BUILDING PATIOS

If you can forget for a minute how much you want the patio already to be done, building it can be fun. Tools that seem awkward at first soon have your hands learning the best way to use them. You'll get a rhythm going; the bricks will start to go onto the sand in the most efficient way, and you'll be moving with ease as you empty the wheelbarrow and reposition the twine. As your confidence grows and the project takes shape, you may find yourself working into twilight to see one more section done. Set things up right, and you'll likely find yourself a little sad when the job's done.

TOOLS Working with good tools eliminates much of the flickering annoyance that can bog down even a small construction project. Invest in a wide steel measuring tape that's at least 18 feet long, so you can get the patio dimensions marked out in one pass, without the tape constantly buckling and rewinding. There's no substitute for a straight-edged spade in making a clean perpendicular trench; any other kind leaves irritating ridges. A shovel with a D-shaped handle is most comfortable for moving sand and gravel. An 8- or 10-foot piece of two-by-four, absolutely straight, will make leveling a large area simple; just place the carpenter's level on top of it.

If you're laying pavers or stones or brick, start out with thick comfortable gloves, sturdy boots, and kneepads. And have a heavy-duty wheelbarrow that you can march around and empty easily. To tamp a sand or gravel foundation properly, you need a special tool—either a hand-held tamper, which is a heavy metal plate on a long handle, or a water-fillable drum roller, or a vibrator-plate compactor, sometimes called a power tamper. Once you have it on site, the plate compactor is by far the fastest means of tamping. Most tool rental outlets have drum rollers and plate compactors.

CUTTING BRICK AND FLAGSTONE ∞ A circular saw with a diamond blade is a tool worth renting if you have to cut much brick, concrete paver, or stone, because it's so fast. For health reasons, be sure to wear gloves, safety goggles, and a proper dust mask while using the saw. To make most efficient use of the rental, mark the brick, paver, or stone ahead of time, using chalk or a grease pencil and a guide board to get a straight edge.

Some professionals use a grinder with a 4½-inch diamond blade (a smaller tool than a circular saw) or a water-cooled masonry saw. You might also use a masonry blade on a circular saw if that's what you have, but the blade will wear quickly. Brick cutters are also available from rental outlets.

The best tool is worth finding, particularly if you are laying flagstones. Flagstone patios look great when the stones speak to one another, a straight edge in one stone following a straight edge in its neighbor, or a concave edge against a convex edge, and when the gaps between the stones are fairly uniform; both usually require some stone trimming or very carefully chosen stones. To fit a stone before trimming it, lay the edge of the neighboring stone over it, and mark a suitable cutting line. To fill an awkward space between laid stones, mark the outline onto paper, cut out the shape, lay it on top of one or two stones, and trace the trim lines.

If you need only a few cut bricks, pavers, or stones and the lines are simple, you can do the cutting by hand using a brick set (a wide chisel) and a hand sledgehammer. Place the brick, paver, or stone on a firm surface. Mark the cut lines on all sides of it, score along the lines with the brick set, center the brick set on the cut line (for flagstone, place a piece of pipe or scrap wood under the stone near the cut line, so that the end of the stone to be trimmed overhangs the pipe or wood), and tap the brick set sharply with the sledge to make the break. Wear gloves and safety goggles to protect yourself from flying chips of masonry. Expect to waste a few stones or bricks as you discover what kind of strike or tap makes a clean break.

CLEARING ROOTS AND WEEDS ∞ Some tree roots, blackberry roots, and bamboo roots will crack a concrete patio. They'll make a hill out of mortared brick and reclaim gravel in the first year. Check a plant encyclopedia if you're in any doubt, and avoid paving close to anything described as having aggressive or invasive roots. If you're paving close to a tree, you can expect some heaving eventually. Gravel is a good choice in such a situation. The odd root can push through the surface without causing damage, and once it's clearly visible, so people won't trip, it makes a beautiful detail.

Clear the patio area of weeds, paying particular attention to crabgrass, couch grass, Bermuda grass, bindweed, oxalis, and any other virulent perennial weed. Water the patio area after clearing the weeds, and wait a few weeks for the dormant weed seeds to sprout. Reweed and water, wait a month, and weed the patio area again. Once the patio is laid, if weeds appear, clear them quickly; don't give them a chance to flower and reseed.

A layer of landscape fabric laid on the bottom of the excavation, underneath your patio materials, may prevent weeds from growing up from the subsoil, but very few of the builders of the projects in this book used it, because weeds are likely to appear anyway from seeds blown onto the patio surface. If you decide to lay it, choose a superporous material so that water will drain quickly through it. To plant through it, make two slits in the form of an X, fold back the corners of the fabric, make a planting hole, and fold the fabric back over the rootball when the plant is in the ground. You must be especially vigilant about clearing the weeds that will inevitably appear despite the fabric. If you leave them until they have good root systems, it's hard to weed without pulling up the fabric with the weeds.

GRADING A SLOPE ⌀↘ Patios require a relatively flat area. If your garden slopes, you'll need to cut into the slope to fashion a level area and remove the soil to another part of the garden. Don't be tempted to cut from the hillside on one side of the patio and berm the soil to build up the downhill side. You shouldn't make a patio on fill; sooner or later the foundation will sag there and take the surface of the patio with it. If necessary, continue to grade the area uphill from the patio to prevent eroded soil or runoff from spilling onto the patio. In most situations, it's wise to make a small gravel drainage ditch to carry the water away before it reaches the patio.

MARKING OUT THE PATIO PERIMETER ⌀↘ Balls of mason's twine, which doesn't stretch much, and lumber stakes (one-by-ones or one-by-twos) are the simplest tools for marking out a square or rectangular patio. Use a separate ball of twine to mark each edge of the patio, so that you can adjust them separately and don't have to restring the whole perimeter if one comes loose. Place the stakes about a foot beyond the patio perimeter, so that they don't get in your way when you're excavating or installing edgings.

To check that the corners are square, do one of three things: Measure the two diagonals between the four corners (they should be the same length). Or place a builder's framing square at each corner. Or check each corner using the 3, 4, 5 triangle method: measure 3 feet along the twine in one direction, measure 4 feet in the other direction, and the diagonal between the two points should be 5 feet. If you are placing a patio alongside a building, correct the corners at the building before checking the others. When everything is square, make sure the stakes are hammered firmly into the ground.

To make a perfectly circular patio, use a piece of twine and two lumber stakes. Hammer a nail partway into the top of each stake, and tie the twine to the nails so that the distance between the stakes when the twine is taut is equal to the radius of the circle. For example, for a patio 10 feet across, the distance between the stakes should be 5 feet. Hammer one stake into the ground at the center of the patio. Keeping the twine taut, draw the patio perimeter in the dirt with the tip of the other stake. This method also works for creating smooth patio curves.

To mark out an irregularly shaped patio, use construction chalk or a water-based marking paint available in spray cans. Keep the lines simple.

CHECKING FOR POOR DRAINAGE ⌀⌀ If the soil under your patio has severe drainage problems, in heavy rains water may pool up through the foundation and flood the patio surface. It's a simple task to check the likelihood of such flooding: Before you excavate the patio, dig a hole roughly 12 inches around and 12 inches deep, and fill it with water. Let it drain, and then refill it. If it fails to drain the second time within twelve hours, you have poor drainage. In all but the most serious cases, you may solve this problem by using the deepest foundation recommended in the patio instructions (see page 115 for calculating amounts of extra material you'll need), but if you have any concerns consult a landscape architect or an experienced contractor who knows the soils in your area.

PROVIDING FOR SURFACE DRAINAGE ❧ The foundation for the patio may provide a sufficient method of drainage, especially if the patio surface is porous and you make a deep foundation. In some situations, however—if you live in an area of high rainfall or heavy storms, your soil doesn't drain well, and the patio surface is more solid than permeable—you may need a drainage system. The simplest is a narrow, gravel-filled ditch on the patio edge, with perforated drainpipe buried in the gravel and laid on a slight slope to take the water away from the patio. Be sure to channel the water so that it doesn't cause erosion or collect around the house foundations or a neighbor's property. If you plan to make a patio by cutting into a steep slope, consult a landscape architect about runoff and erosion problems.

In every situation, it makes sense to slope the patio at least 1 inch every 8 feet, so that it sheds rainwater and runoff, and to lay the patio 1 inch above the surrounding soil level, so dirt doesn't wash onto it during a rain shower.

A PROPER BASE ❧ Most patios can be laid in two ways: onto sand or gravel, or onto a concrete slab. The simpler method is to lay a patio onto sand or gravel. It is not as permanent a base as concrete, but it is very durable and works well, provided the edges of the patio are contained if necessary and the base is thoroughly compacted. Professionals often choose sand and gravel instead of concrete just because it isn't permanent—if a brick or stone pops above the surface, you can pick it up, smooth the base, and re-lay it. A patio laid on sand or gravel also looks more informal, and you can plant into it. (Always use angular, mechanically crushed gravel or rock for a patio foundation, never round, water-washed stone, such as pea gravel, which scatters instead of packing down tight.)

Laying a concrete slab is heavy work and not easy for an inexperienced person to get right the first time. It may also prove troublesome in the long term. Concrete can crack and heave, knocking the mortared surface out of kilter. Once this happens, it's very difficult to repair. The patios in this book are built on a sand or gravel foundation.

How deep a base to make depends on your soil: how well it drains and how stable it is. Do the drainage test described on page 28 if you're unsure of your drainage. If the soil drains well, next consider the soil stability. In Florida, the South, and southern and coastal California, soils are generally stable, and patios do not require the deep base needed for patios laid in the northern half of the country, where the ground freezes hard in winter. If your soil contains a lot of clay or sand, it probably isn't reliably stable throughout the year. With these two pieces of information—drainage and stability—in hand, you can follow the recommendations given for each patio, at the beginning of the "How to Do It" text. If you suspect you have a soil stability problem, especially if you're building on a slope, consult a geotechnical engineer.

EXCAVATING ◐◑ Before you begin to dig, spend a few minutes setting up lines of twine to use as an excavation guide. String at least two or three lines of twine across the patio area so that the twine sits at the desired finished height of the patio—for example, 1 inch above the soil level (see page 29) or 1 to 3 inches below the kitchen floor if you're building off the house (always make the patio lower than the adjoining indoor floor). If you have strung perimeter lines (see page 27), adjust those to the proper height. If the patio adjoins the house, set the twine up correctly there first. Use a line level, a small tool that clips onto twine, to make sure the twine is level between the stakes.

Now adjust the twine to take account of the small slope you want to create so that water will drain off the patio. The slope should be at least 1 inch every 8 feet, or ¼ inch every 2 feet. Calculate how great a pitch you need, and on the downslope side of the patio, lower the twine on the stakes by that amount. With a knife, score the position of the twine on all the stakes, so you can reset the twine easily if it slips while you are excavating.

With the twine now marking the finished sloping surface of the patio, you can excavate to the required depth using the twine as a reference. To calculate the required depth, add the thickness of your paving to the depth of the base materials. Say, for example, you are laying stone 2 inches thick on a 1-inch sand bed over 4 inches of gravel; then excavate 7 inches below the twine.

On all but the smallest patios, it helps to have a grid of twine so that you have a measuring reference even at the patio center. Set up lines of twine every 6 feet, making sure lines running down the slope have the pitch built in.

Once you've excavated the patio area, you can use the perimeter lines as a guide for positioning the edging. Place the edging so it just touches the twine, and it'll be level with the patio surface; lower the twine at each stake by ½ or 1 inch if you want the edging to sit below the patio surface.

THE EDGING DECISION ✐✐ An edging is a device for containment. It helps keep soil or lawn grasses or ground covers from creeping onto the patio and paving material from sliding into the flower beds. In extremely informal situations, an edging is unnecessary: perhaps it really doesn't matter if gravel crosses into the beds or forget-me-nots germinate in the patio and the surface sags or tilts as the edges move. In most situations, however, especially if you want the patio surface to stay even, be safe, and last a long time, the integrity of the patio must be protected, and an edging contributes to that.

Whether you need an edging depends on what's happening beneath and around your patio surface. If the patio surface is well tamped onto a solid deep base surrounded by soil that's stable in all seasons, then you can perhaps simply pack outside soil firmly around your patio edges. It's a matter of common sense. Think about what might shift the patio surface: it will move if heavy storms flood the surface or wash the sand away from underneath the surface, but if you have arranged for excellent drainage, then that won't happen.

The patio surface is less likely to move if the paving units are large; often in the projects in this book, the ingredients list calls for particularly large pieces of stone, because they are far more stable than small pieces. This is especially important on the patio edges. A deep, compacted base also helps to stabilize the patio surface. If you extend the base beyond the patio edges, the portion under the patio edge is less likely to be eroded. If you think you might be skimping on base materials, you have more reason to edge.

Bear in mind that a sand bed by itself isn't a stable foundation—its particles are round and slip. The primary purpose of a sand bed is to provide a surface that you can smooth, so the patio surface is even. Some landscape architects use a thin bed of sand for this reason, or set paving on a bed of fines (angular gravel particles that compact better than sand).

As a general rule of thumb, standard brick needs an edging. So does gravel if you want to maintain a clean edge. Large, heavy units of paving may not need an edging, especially if the base is deep and other conditions are favorable. Finally, decide how upset you'd be if the surface warped or stones snapped. Perhaps a little disintegration would add to the informal look of the space. But if it would make the surface unsafe, don't take risks. A last word of caution: an edging is in no way a substitute for proper grading or drainage; it's only an aid in keeping things in place, and it probably won't last forever.

EDGING CHOICES ◦◦◦ Wood edgings of two-by-fours—or two-by-sixes for a heavily trafficked patio with a deep base—are relatively inexpensive and easy to install. Most woods rot quickly in damp soils, so always choose heartwood cedar or redwood for the stakes and boards, or use pressure-treated woods. At a corner, first nail the two pieces of edging together to make an L, then place them into the excavation, and nail them to the stakes.

For curves, use wooden benderboard: nail one piece to a set of stakes that defines the curve, and build up the desired thickness with additional lengths of benderboard, nailing them together and to the stakes. Or use recycled-plastic benderboard, the sturdiest kind, or metal edging if you can find it. For informal situations, edge a patio with small rocks set firmly into the soil.

If you are laying brick, or pieces of concrete or stone, consider installing an edging in two phases. Edge two adjoining sides of the patio first and start work from that corner. When you've finished laying the patio, install the edging on the remaining two sides, butting it tightly against the paving. If you install all the edging at the beginning, you may find you have to cut the bricks to get them to fit exactly within the perimeter. However, you might tack all the edging boards into place at the start of the project if they will help you level and screed the base materials.

Four-by-fours make a convenient level edging for a patio that borders a lawn. Position the wood flush with the lawn (where the grasses meet the soil surface), so that you can run the mower with one wheel on the edging.

Pre-formed plastic edgings are available for brick and concrete pavers. A stiff, restraining band sits against the bricks or pavers and keeps them in line; at the base of the band, below soil level, are plastic loops for spikes that you hammer into the ground.

Pay particular attention to the points where people will walk over the patio edge, where the patio meets the house doors, for example, or leads onto a path. Secure these edges well, resting them in a base of mortar for safety, if they might become uneven or unsteady.

SCREEDING A SAND BED ◦◦◦ *Screeding* a sand bed means smoothing and leveling the sand until there are no high or low spots and the bed is firm, so the paving will sit flat on top of it. You dampen and tamp the sand bed before screeding it.

A piece of two-by-four lumber is the simplest screeding board; you pull it over the sand in a sawing motion. To keep the surface of the bed level, or lightly pitched for drainage (see page 29), it's helpful to run the board along guides. One system is to lay two pipes or poles on sections of the patio base before pouring the sand and guide the screeding board along those. The outer diameter of the pipes should be equal to the depth of the sand bed. Check that the tops of the pipes are at the right grade by measuring down from the excavation twine lines. Once you have screeded one section, move one of the poles and screed the next section. Patch the spaces left by the poles with sand.

Alternatively, if you have installed wood edgings for your patio, you can make a screeding board that rests on those. You'll need a 4-foot length of two-by-four lumber and a piece of plywood 3½ feet long and as wide as the two-by-four (4 inches if the lumber is unfinished, less if finished) plus the thickness of your paving material. Lay the two-by-four on top of the plywood, aligning one edge so that the ends of the two-by-four overhang 3 inches for handles.

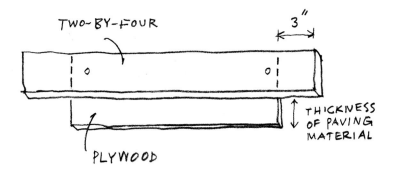

Nail the plywood to the two-by-four. When you're ready to screed, rest one handle on the perimeter edging, and set a temporary board or pipe on the sand bed as described in the paragraph above, to guide the other handle.

Screed several times, tamping after each pass. The firmer the base, the more stable the surface will be.

To check that the sand bed is level, place a carpenter's level on it. If you're building on a slight slope, as recommended, to allow for good drainage, you'll need to attach a piece of wood on one end of your level to compensate for your grade (if your level is 4 feet long and your drop is 1 inch in 8 feet, you'll need a ½-inch block on the downhill end).

BUYING AND TRANSPORTING PAVING MATERIALS

Garden centers and nurseries usually have only the smallest choice of paving materials. Check the Yellow Pages under these categories: Brick, Building Materials, Cement, Concrete Products, Landscaping Equipment and Supplies, Lumber–Retail, Lumber–Used, Quarries, Rock, Sawdust, Sod, Stone–Natural, Tile. Contractors and landscape architects buy from these sources.

Once you've found the patio surface material, the foundation materials, and the edging material, calculate how much you need of each (the recipes indicate quantities; if you're adapting a recipe, see "Calculating Quantities of Materials" on page 115 to work out what you'll need). Purchase a little extra of everything, in case you have to do repair work in the future. Paving materials are heavy; if you plan on picking them up yourself, first calculate the weight roughly with the supplier, and check that your vehicle is rated for that load weight. Decide on a delivery site as close as possible to the new patio. If gravel or sand is being dumped loose, spread a tarp across the ground, so you won't be forever trying to pick the last bits of stone out of the grass.

BUYING PLANTS ♠ At the nursery, choose strong healthy plants, with no evidence of pests or disease, no anemic-looking leaves, and no roots tangling out of the bottom of the pot. Take the ones with the most shoots from the base, or the most branches; leave the thin spindly samples, even if they are in flower. For the fastest cover, choose the largest plants if you like, though these will be more expensive. Sometimes it's not worth the extra expense, because smaller plants will take off faster when planted.

Before you leave the nursery, buy a soil mix specifically designed for containers if you are planting in containers. Also check the plant label for special soil requirements for that plant. If a plant needs rich soil, and you haven't recently dug compost or manure into your soil, pick some up from the nursery, and dig it in before you plant. If the plant label mentions well-drained soil and you know your ground is often soggy or clayey, choose a different plant. Ask the nursery person to recommend a substitute; consider the flower color, the plant height and spread, and the foliage color and texture.

PLANTING THE PLANTS ♠ Plant as soon as you can. Dig a hole as deep as the pot and a little wider. If you are planting in gravel, first remove the layer of gravel from the planting area. If you are planting in the cracks between paving pieces, first scoop out any sand packed there.

The bottom of the planting hole is best left flat for perennials; for shrubs and trees, dig a trench around the perimeter of the bottom, leaving a mound in the center for the plant to sit on.

Water the plant in its pot, and then gently tip it out into your hands. Plants in cell-packs can be pushed up and out by poking your thumb underneath each cell. If a plant doesn't slip easily out of a plastic pot, slide a knife between the soil and the pot, tip the pot onto its side, and tap the base of the pot, holding the plant by its stem. Trees sometimes won't slip out of heavy plastic or metal pots without cutting the pot—make a slit from the rim to the base. Be a little careful with the knife, so as not to cut through big roots.

Take a hard look at the plant's rootball. Many plants have been in nurseries too long, and the roots have had nowhere to grow but around and around into a dense mat. Rootballs like these slide out of the pot in one solid mass; if there was growing room to spare, loose soil will tumble from the pot. To help plants with matted rootballs get off to a good start, do some surgery. With your thumb or a sharp knife, score into the rootball, from top to bottom, at several places around the circumference. With your fingers, pry the roots loose, breaking small thin roots as you need to, but being careful not to snap thick roots. Freed from the tight tangle, the roots will now quickly grow out into fresh soil. Prune off any rotten or diseased roots.

Place the plant in the planting hole. The top of the rootball must be slightly above the soil surface, at least 1 inch above for trees. If you're planting a tree that needs staking, drive the stake deep into the ground on one side of the rootball. Fill in around the rootball with the soil you removed to dig the hole, packing it firmly and lifting the plant if necessary to keep it above the soil level. Handle the plant always by the main stem.

Press the soil firmly around the plant. The soil must make contact with the roots; if there are air pockets around the roots, they'll die. Make a watering moat, and water the plant generously. If you're staking a tree, loop the tie from stake to tree loosely. Until the plant starts to produce new growth and is obviously established, water regularly. The soil should never dry out 2 inches below the surface. Drought-tolerant plants need less frequent watering once they are established. Keep watering other plants regularly.

OUTDOOR DINING ROOMS

Setting the table with linen and silver and inviting people to leave the comforts of the living room for the unpredictable environment of the outdoors causes a frisson of excitement even on a sunny day. The thrill increases if you use your best fragile glass and china—in the manner of an outdoor wedding or a colonial Victorian tea. There's always a flutter when people dressed in their finest shoes and silk, sally boldly into the sun, the hosts locked in a dare with fate that the weather won't change.

For smaller parties, with less safety in numbers, you might make your guests feel more comfortable by providing shelter. Place the patio next to the garden wall or the house and provide a ceiling of vines or garden umbrellas. For a really cozy meal, install a fireplace with the grate raised off the floor so people can gaze into the flames.

Just as romantic as formal tablecloths shadowed with the glow of the setting sun is a log picnic table under an arbor of wild roses away from the house. It's a call to pack up a sandwich and go down through the garden on an adventure, to see how long you and your friends can stay away from the comforts of home and be idle among the petals drifting to the floor.

To be comfortable, outdoor dining rooms need generous space; allow plenty of room for table, chairs, and cooking and serving equipment. Be sure the chairs are exquisitely comfortable and that they don't wobble on an uneven floor.

GRANITE CHIPS
IN GRASS SQUARE

Because spring comes late and summer is short, the table is set up in a clearing to catch every hour of sun. In late June it's warm enough to sit outside for as long as the sun stays clear of the clouds. The light runs in silver streams across the lake down the hill, shining through the trees; and a cool wind tosses the spring blossoms about. The clematis-covered fence provides some shelter to the patio. The fountain grasses riffle now and then, and the clear light warms the seats and glints off the chips of gray and white granite on the floor.

HOW TO DO IT ✦✦

This patio includes a foundation of 4 inches of crushed rock and a surface of 2 inches of gravel. The patio is edged with wood two-by-fours. In a dry climate and freely draining soil, you could lay just 2 inches of crushed rock; in poorly draining soils, lay 6 inches. The patio floor is the easy part of the project. At the entrance to the patio are low granite plinths, which need concrete footings; have a contractor install the footings unless you are experienced at concrete work.

Before you start to build, check the sections on grading and drainage, pages 27 and 28–29.

Mark out the patio perimeter with the twine and stakes. Make it an elegant 6 yards square (the table is 3½ feet across). Set the twine ½ inch above the finished patio surface (see page 30) so you can use it to place the edging two-by-fours, which sit ½ inch higher than the gravel.

Excavate inside the patio perimeter to a depth of 6 inches. Firm the bottom of the excavation if you've disturbed the soil while digging.

Drive the stake one-by-twos into the sides of the excavation, outside the twine, at intervals of 8 feet. Position the edging two-by-fours so that they touch the twine, and nail them to the stakes, holding or wedging the stakes firmly upright during the hammering. Then hammer more stakes against the edging on the inside of the patio, to help prevent the edging from warping. Space them at intervals of 8 feet, between the outside stakes. Saw off any protruding stakes on the outside flush with the edging; on the inside, saw the stakes 1 inch below the edging, so they'll be hidden by the gravel.

Spread 4 inches of crushed rock into the bottom of the excavation, moisten it, and pack it down with the tamper.

Spread 2 inches of gravel on the surface, moisten it, and pack it down with the tamper. Firm the soil outside against the patio edges.

Plant the fountain grasses 4 feet apart along the patio perimeter, 2 feet back from the edge.

To make the stone plinths, mark out an area roughly 18 inches square (depending on the fit of the stones and allowing for 1-inch mortar joints between them). Have a contractor install concrete footings for the plinths. They'll need to be several inches thick, much thicker if the ground freezes. Build the plinths once the footings have cured.

Wearing the rubber gloves, make a batch of mortar, and spread a 1-inch-

Moderately inexpensive
Easy in part (see text)
Location: Sun

Tools
Twine and stakes
Measuring tape
Straight-edged spade, for digging
Hammer
Saw
Shovel, for spreading materials
Hose
Hand-held tamper, or rented water-
    fillable roller or vibrator-plate
    compactor
Planting trowel
Rubber gloves
Mortar mixing box
Mason's trowel
Rubber mallet
Sponge
Piece of plywood, for raking joints

Ingredients
Redwood, heartwood cedar, or
    pressure-treated wood two-by-fours,
    for edging, length of patio perimeter
Stake one-by-twos, 18 inches long,
    1 stake per 4 feet of perimeter,
    and nails
Crushed rock, ¾-inch, 4½ cubic yards
Gravel, crushed granite, ⅝-inch, no fines,
    2¼ cubic yards
Fountain grasses (Pennisetum
    alopecuroides), 1 per 4 feet of patio
    perimeter
Stone for 2 plinths, approx. 10 cubic feet;
    choose roughly trimmed blocks,
    preferably the same type of stone
    as the gravel
Mortar materials: 1 part portland cement
    and 3 parts sand, or a packaged Type
    M mortar with no lime

Maintenance
Water grasses regularly until established,
    then only in dry season
Rake gravel regularly
Top up gravel as necessary

thick layer on the footing, using the mason's trowel. Set the first layer of stones into the mortar bed, leaving 1-inch gaps between them and tapping each stone gently with the mallet to bed it. Scoop mortar into the gaps between the stones. Clean up spilled mortar from the face of the stone with a wet sponge as you work. Spread a mortar bed on top of the stones, and set the next layer of stones in the mortar; repeat the process until the plinth is 18 to 20 inches high. Before the mortar sets, use a piece of plywood to rake out the joints to a depth of ½ to ¾ inches.

GRASS WAVE, TOSSED BRICK

The lawn runs up the slope from Lake Washington over the brick terrace like a wave that has crested and is beginning to recede. The large dining terrace is left high and dry, only drops of green moss and bluegrass penetrating the closely butted bricks. Along the rest of the house, a stretch of path runs above the tide line to another, smaller, terrace with a second table and chairs.

The landscape architect, Rich Haag, likes to break down the hard lines between materials using natural soft lines of flow. As he was making the brick pattern in the lawn he had in mind the game of tossing cards into a cowboy hat—the cards fall thickest closest to the hat and more sporadically farther away.

HOW TO DO IT ∾

This patio is laid on a foundation of 4 inches of gravel and 2 inches of sand. If your soil freezes hard or drains poorly, lay 6 to 8 inches of gravel. The joints between the bricks are filled with sand. There is no edging; the land here is stable, and the bricks are large (8 inches square), so they are less likely to shift than regular bricks. A little irregularity in the surface may develop over time. See page 31 to decide whether you should install an edging.

Before you start to build, check the sections on grading and drainage, pages 27 and 28–29.

Mark out the patio perimeter with the twine and stakes. Wrap the terrace along one or two sides of your house; make it broad enough for a dining area outside the kitchen, plan for a lounger or two off a bedroom perhaps, and narrow it to path width in the places between. Make all the spaces very generous.

On the lawn side, establish the perimeter as the last, or almost the last, solid line of brick; you'll set the spray of bricks in the lawn individually. Make the edge of the terrace against the house soft also; except where the terrace meets the house doors, make flower beds with irregular edges between the house and the brick. Set the twine at the level of the finished patio surface (see page 30) so you can use it to place the brick.

Excavate below the twine to a depth of 6 inches plus the depth of the brick. Firm the bottom of the excavation if you've disturbed the soil while digging. Spread 4 inches of gravel into the bottom of the excavation, moisten it, and pack it down with the tamper.

Spread 2 inches of sand over the gravel base. Dampen the sand and tamp it, then screed it thoroughly (see page 32) by drawing the two-by-four across it, and tamp again. Check with the level that the sand bed is even.

Where the terrace meets the house, insert a strip of flashing between the brick and the house walls.

Starting at a corner, lay the bricks in a running bond pattern as shown, butting them against one another. Place the bricks directly on top of the sand; don't wedge or push them in. To keep the sand bed level and undisturbed, avoid kneeling on it directly; place the sheet of polystyrene or plywood on the bed, and kneel on that. Settle each brick on top of the sand by tapping it with the mallet. With the level, check that it's flush with the other bricks; if necessary, lift the brick and remove some sand or add a little more underneath it.

Moderately expensive
Moderately easy
Location: Sun or light shade

Tools

Twine and stakes
Measuring tape
Straight-edged spade, for digging
Shovel, for spreading materials
Hand-held tamper, or rented water-
    fillable roller or vibrator-plate
    compactor
Hose
Piece of straight two-by-four, for leveling
    sand
Level
Sheet of thick polystyrene or plywood,
    for kneeling on sand
Rubber mallet
Broom
Knife, for cutting turf

Ingredients

Gravel, sharp-edged, ⅝- or ¾-inch, 3¼
    cubic feet per square yard of terrace
Builder's sand, 1¾ cubic feet per square
    yard of terrace, including sand for
    joints
Flashing, length of areas where patio
    meets house walls
Bricks, 8 inches square, approx. 22 per
    square yard (includes almost 10
    percent extra for breakage), plus
    bricks for the spray in the lawn

Maintenance

Refill gaps between bricks with sand
    periodically

To finish the patio, spread dry sand over the bricks, and sweep it into the joints. Keep spreading and sweeping until the joints are full. Sprinkle the surface with a very fine spray from the hose to settle the sand in the joints. Top up the sand as necessary, and water again. The firmly settled sand locks the bricks in place, so be sure to fill the joints well.

To make the pattern of bricks in the lawn, cut out the existing turf with a knife, brick by brick. Excavate to a depth of 2 inches plus the thickness of the brick, lay a 2-inch layer of sand, dampen and tamp it, and lay the brick as described earlier. Think about the way cards would fall around a hat: place lots of bricks close to the terrace, and fewer the farther you move into the grass. Keep the stray bricks in the same running bond grid as the terrace bricks. Lift an occasional brick from the edge of the terrace, gently remove some of the sand and gravel without disturbing the foundation of the terrace, fill the hole with garden soil, and lay a square of turf on the surface. Water the replaced turf regularly until it is established.

WARM RED BRICK AND
SMOKE TREE

This patio contains built-in warmth and liveliness. It's convivial because of its colors. Pink-red brick, rich brown-red furniture, and a purple-red smoke tree are contrasted with a green hedge. Even though the reds are subtle, they pop—because they are on the opposite side of the color wheel from green—and give the patio presence.

As well as contrast, there's harmony here, which is warm and easy on the eye. Whereas white furniture would have made the new brick seem harsh, the mahogany stain on the wood brings out the pink hues in the brick, and the smoke tree adds more warm rich colors with its plum-purple leaves and rosy pink puffs of faded blossoms. Seen against the glow, even the white flowers look warm.

HOW TO DO IT ∞

This patio is laid on a foundation of 4 inches of crushed rock and 1 inch of sand. If your soil freezes hard or drains poorly, lay 6 to 8 inches of crushed rock. The bricks and sand are contained by an invisible plastic edging. The joints between the bricks are filled with sand.

Before you start to build, check the sections on grading and drainage, pages 27 and 28–29.

Note that the herringbone pattern requires a standard paving brick that is exactly half as wide as it is long and many precisely cut half bricks at the patio edges. For a patio this large, consider renting a tool to cut the bricks. Try out the herringbone pattern, as described later, to make sure the bricks work. Once you've got the hang of it, cut some bricks in half with the brick-cutting tool; you'll need fifty-something half bricks, three for every 4 feet or so of patio perimeter.

Mark out the patio perimeter with the twine and stakes. This patio is a generous 6 yards square (the table is 4½ feet across), which allows room for a side table, a bench, and additional chairs. Set the twine at the level of the finished patio surface (see page 30) so you can use it to place the brick.

Excavate below the twine to a depth of 5 inches plus the depth of the brick. Firm the bottom of the excavation if you've disturbed the soil while digging.

Spread 4 inches of crushed rock into the bottom of the excavation, moisten it, and pack it down with the tamper.

Place the plastic edging along two adjoining sides of the excavation. Install it with the top edge below the twine, so it won't be visible once the bricks are in place. Secure the edging with the stakes.

Spread 1 inch of sand over the crushed rock base. Dampen the sand and tamp it, then screed it thoroughly (see page 32) by drawing the two-by-four across it, and tamp again. Check with the level that the sand bed is even.

Starting at the corner with the edging in place, make a plain brick border for the herringbone pattern by laying bricks side by side, long sides touching, along the two edges of the patio. Butt the bricks, so there are no gaps between them. Place the bricks directly on top of the sand; don't wedge or push them in. To keep the sand bed level and undisturbed, avoid kneeling directly on it; place the sheet of polystyrene or plywood on the bed, and kneel on that. Settle each brick on top of the sand by tapping it with the mallet. With the level, check that it's flush with the other bricks; if necessary, lift the brick and remove some sand or add a little more underneath it.

Moderately inexpensive
Moderately difficult
Location: Sun

Tools

Brick-cutting tool (see page 26)
Twine and stakes
Measuring tape
Straight-edged spade, for digging
Shovel, for spreading materials
Hose
Hand-held tamper, or rented water-fillable roller or vibrator-plate compactor
Hammer
Piece of straight two-by-four, for leveling sand
Level
Sheet of thick polystyrene or plywood, for kneeling on sand
Rubber mallet
Framing square
Broom

Ingredients

Bricks, exactly twice as long as wide, approx. 1,620, or 5 per square foot, including 10 percent for breakage and future repairs
Crushed rock, ⅝-inch minus, 4½ cubic yards
Plastic preformed invisible edging for brick, with stakes, 24 yards
Builder's sand, 1¼ cubic yards, including sand for joints
Purple smoke tree (*Cotinus coggygria* 'Pink Champagne')

Maintenance

Water smoke tree regularly until established, and then less frequently
Refill joints with sand as necessary

Once you've laid the brick border along the two sides of the patio you've edged, go back to the corner where you started and begin the herringbone pattern: Lay the first two bricks, one vertical, right in the corner, one horizontal beside it, to make an L. Lay the third and fourth bricks into the corner

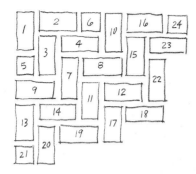

made by the first two bricks, again in an L. You'll see now that you need two half bricks next to the first two bricks. Lay those next, then go back to the corner made by the third and fourth bricks, lay another L there, and fill to the edge of the patio using a full brick on each side (one will be horizontal, one vertical). Go back to the middle, lay another L, and fill to the edge with two Ls, using full bricks. The next time you fill to the patio edges, you'll need half bricks. Continue the pattern, always going back to the center and filling to the edges. Use the framing square to keep the Ls square.

When you reach the third and fourth sides of the patio and can see where the bricks end, install the plastic edging on those two sides, and lay the brick border.

To finish the patio, spread dry sand over the bricks, and sweep it into the joints. Keep spreading and sweeping until the joints are full. Sprinkle the surface with a very fine spray from the hose to settle the sand in the joints. Top up the sand as necessary, and water again. Firm the soil outside against the patio edging.

Plant the purple smoke tree alongside the patio, 3 feet from the edge.

COLORED CONCRETE, LOST MODESTY

Originally the back door of this city property faced the back gate honest and square, and the garden looked suitably modest, just like the ones next door. Then landscape architect David Yakish swung a colored concrete path out at a diagonal into the back of the garden, taking your eye off the gate. At the end of the path, he created this large, exuberant patio.

The lines of the paving are cleverly drawn. The path runs diagonal to the house but parallel to the face of the home office beyond the patio; the patio, mostly circular, is centered on both the bay window of the office and the back door of the house. The boundaries of the garden have been put out of sight among the flowers.

HOW TO DO IT ⌘ This concrete patio was poured onto a gravel foundation between wooden forms, which were removed when the concrete had set; the concrete was stamped after it was poured and then colored with terra-cotta stain when it had cured. The foundation, forms, and staining are the moderately easy parts of the project; unless you have experience working with concrete, have ready-mix concrete delivered and pumped to the patio site, and hire a contractor to pour and stamp the concrete. Laying concrete is heavy work and costly to fix if it goes wrong.

The concrete rests on 4 inches of gravel. In a frost-free climate and freely draining soil, you could lay just 2 inches of gravel; if your soil freezes hard or drains poorly, lay 8 inches. (In very frosty areas, consider ordering concrete that includes an air-entraining agent.)

Before you start to build, check the sections on grading and drainage, pages 27 and 28–29.

Mark out the patio perimeter with the twine and stakes. First decide on the position of the table, centering it on an architectural feature, such as a bay window or the back door, and an element in the garden, such as a path. Allow at least 5 feet around each side of the table, so people can take their seats comfortably. Shape the patio to marry it to strong surrounding lines that you'd like to emphasize or integrate (if you want to lose the garden boundaries, make sure the final shape does not follow those lines). This patio, for example, is basically circular, to mimic the bay window, but at one corner, away from the bay window, there's a square edge that relates to the straight edge of the path that joins the patio there. Keep the shape as simple as possible (later you can place sculpture, boulders, or mounding plants to distract the eye from small awkward places). If there are no strong lines except the straight boundary lines, perhaps use a circle and create a semicircle of trees or clipped hedging off to one side of it. Set the twine at the level of the finished patio surface (see page 30) so you can use it to place the forms.

Excavate below the twine to a depth of 8 inches. Excavate a few inches beyond the perimeter so you have room to place the wooden forms. Firm the bottom of the excavation if you've disturbed the soil while digging.

Spread 4 inches of gravel into the excavation, moisten it, and pack it down with the tamper. Check with the level that the gravel bed is even.

Make the forms for the concrete. For straight edges, use two-by-fours (be

Moderately expensive
Moderately easy in part (see text)
Location: Sun or shade

Tools
Twine and stakes
Measuring tape
Straight-edged spade, for digging
Shovel, for spreading materials
Hose
Hand-held tamper or rented water-
    fillable roller
Level
Hammer
Brace (optional)
Saw, if necessary, to level protruding
    stakes
Paintbrush, for applying form-release
    agent
Wire cutter or heavy pliers, for cutting
    mesh (optional; see text)
Plastic sheet, to cover curing concrete
Brush, for cleaning concrete, if necessary
Paint roller or pump sprayer
Paintbrush, for applying sealant

Ingredients
Gravel, sharp-edged, ⅝-inch minus,
    3 cubic feet per square yard of patio
For the forms:
    Two-by-four unfinished lumber or
        flexible plywood or sheet metal
        or benderboard, length of patio
        perimeter (see text)
    6-inch pieces of one-by-four, to use
        as splices (see text)
    Double-headed 3 ½-inch nails
    Stake two-by-twos, 18 inches long
Form-release agent
Wire reinforcing mesh with 6-inch grid,
    to almost cover patio area
Stones, to support mesh
Wire, to tie overlapping pieces of wire
    mesh (optional; see text)
Ready-mix concrete; give patio
    dimensions to supplier
Trisodium phosphate, if necessary (see
    text)
Concrete chemical stain, terra-cotta
Concrete sealant

Maintenance
Apply new coat of stain eventually,
    if necessary

48

sure the lumber is rough; if you buy finished lumber, it will be only 3½ inches wide). To make curving forms, use 4-inch-wide strips of flexible plywood such as ³⁄₁₆-inch paneling, or sheet metal, or wooden benderboard. Lay the forms around the edges of the excavation so the tops just touch the perimeter twine. If there is a gap between the forms and the gravel, spread more gravel and tamp it firmly, or the liquid concrete will slip under the forms.

Where two boards meet along a side, nail a 6-inch piece of one-by-four over the seam, on the outside. Brace the back of the lumber with your foot or a metal brace to keep it upright during nailing. Use double-headed nails, which will make the forms easier to dismantle later.

Hammer stakes on the outside of the forms to secure them. Place a stake on each side of a corner and every 3 feet along the patio edges, every 1½ feet around curves. Drive the stakes deep into the ground, and use at least two nails to nail them to the forms. The stakes must be strong and very secure, or the concrete will push apart the forms. Pay particular attention to the corners and the places where the boards meet. If you can, hammer the stakes below the tops of the forms; otherwise, saw the tops off flush with the forms (the contractor will use the forms to level the concrete, so the stakes mustn't protrude above the forms).

With the paintbrush, grease the insides and tops of the forms with the form-release agent, so that you'll be able to slip the forms away from the concrete when it's set.

Lay the wire reinforcing mesh if you have the tools to cut it. Otherwise have the contractor do it. The wire should cover the patio area to within 2 inches of the forms and sit 2 inches above the gravel, so the mesh is roughly in the middle of the concrete when it's poured. Place stones on the gravel to support the mesh. Cut the mesh to fit. If you need to use more than one piece, overlap the edges by 6 inches, and tie the two layers together with wire.

Before the contractor and concrete arrive, decide on the stamping pattern you want. Note how the pattern in the photograph establishes a place for the table, like a rug. The contractor may be willing to implement your ideas on the spot, but it might be wise to draw a plan of the pattern ahead of time.

The contractor needs to install expansion strips between the patio and any existing structure, such as the house or a solid walkway, so that the concrete patio doesn't crack as it expands and contracts with weather changes. As the concrete is poured, the contractor works it with a shovel or a hoe to remove air bubbles, especially from the corners, then screeds and floats (levels and smooths) the surface; brooms it to give it traction in wet weather; makes the stamping pattern and the jointing grooves, which control cracking as the concrete hardens; and runs the blade of a trowel and an edger around the patio so that the concrete doesn't chip when you remove the forms.

Remove the forms three or four hours after the concrete is poured. Leave the concrete to cure for five days, covering it with the plastic sheet so it doesn't dry out during hot weather.

After thirty days, the concrete is fully cured and ready for staining. First, wash the patio well. If water alone doesn't remove all the marks that have accumulated, clean them off with a warm-water trisodium phosphate solution. Apply the stain with a paint roller or a pump sprayer. Follow the directions on the container for the recommended number of coats. Finish the patio by applying a standard concrete sealant to help protect the color.

ROSE BOWER WITH
FLAGSTONES AND VIOLETS

*An unusual single white Lady Banks'
rose and a porcelain vine have twined
over this rustic bower hidden up the
hillside from an elegant house in the
town. Away from the civilized lawns,
sheltered by trailing greenery, it's a
place for imagining yourself in a hut
in the woods. The light dapples green
through the vines, flickering on the
woodland branches, trunks, and roots
that make up the walls and furniture,
and the floor smells of rich, moist earth
and violets.*

*There's a single peep back out into
the brightly lit world: a window pierced
in a nearby hedge offers an oblique view
of a birdbath on the lawn.*

HOW TO DO IT ✑ The bower's flagstone floor is laid on a foundation of 2 inches of gravel and 2 inches of sand. If your soil freezes hard or drains poorly, lay 6 to 8 inches of gravel. The floor is edged with six-by-six lumber landscape ties.

The patio floor is the moderately easy and inexpensive part of the project. Unless you are experienced in carpentry work, have a contractor build the arbor structure; for a rustic effect, use rough but durable wood, such as redwood or cedar. The landscape architect, Sydney Baumgartner, designed the wall lattice here of mulberry whips. The table base is a bunch of tree roots she salvaged from a beach after a storm and bolted together; the table top and sideboard are made of two-by-sixes with a frame. The sideboard legs are tree trunks. The split birch, willow, and pine chairs were imported from Spain. The frame in the hedge is an old picture frame; it's supported on two legs of two-by-fours and tied to the hedge.

Before you start to build the patio floor, check the sections on grading and drainage, pages 27 and 28–29.

Mark out the perimeter of the floor with the twine and stakes; make it 8 feet wide and 12 feet long for a cozy space just large enough to seat six (the table is 3 feet by 6 feet). Set the twine at the level of the finished patio surface (see page 30) so you can use it to place the edging.

Excavate below the twine to the depth of the ties. Firm the bottom of the excavation if you've disturbed the soil while digging. Lay the landscape ties around the edges of the excavation; saw one tie in two to finish the long sides. The tops of the ties should just touch the twine.

Secure the ties with the rebar: drill a hole 9 to 12 inches from each end of each tie, and hammer a rod of rebar through the hole into the ground.

Spread 2 inches of gravel into the excavation, moisten it, and pack it down with the tamper.

Before you lay the sand bed, spread the flagstones on the gravel and rearrange them until you have the best fit requiring the least amount of cutting. Leave gaps of 1 to 1½ inches between the stones for planting the violets. Trim the stones that need trimming (see page 26), and move all the stones outside the excavation in an orderly way so that you'll remember how to fit them together.

Spread 2 inches of sand over the gravel base. Dampen the sand and tamp it,

Moderately inexpensive in part (see text)
Moderately easy in part (see text)
Location: Sun or light shade

Tools
Twine and stakes
Measuring tape
Straight-edged spade, for digging
Saw
Drill with ¾-inch bit
Hammer
Shovel, for spreading materials
Hose
Hand-held tamper or rented water-
    fillable roller
Stone-cutting tools (see page 26)
Piece of straight two-by-four, for leveling
    sand
Level
Sheet of thick polystyrene or plywood,
    for kneeling on sand
Rubber mallet
Planting trowel

Ingredients
Arbor to cover patio floor (see text)
5 landscape ties, pressure-treated
    six-by-sixes, 8 feet long
12 rebar rods, ¾-inch diameter, at least
    18 inches long
Gravel, sharp-edged, ⅜-inch, ½ cubic
    yard
Flagstones, at least 18 to 30 inches wide,
    and 1½ inches thick, to cover approx.
    100 square feet
Builder's sand, ½ cubic yard
Rich organic soil mix
Violets (Viola), white-flowered, approx.
    100 to 200, in cell packs or flats; the
    smaller the plants are, the better
Lady Banks' rose (Rosa banksiae), white-
    flowering form
Porcelain vine (Ampelopsis brevipeduncu-
    lata)

Maintenance
Water violets regularly
Fertilize violets in very early spring
Prune rose annually once it's established,
    to reduce shading
Clean stone occasionally, if light-colored
    and prone to staining

then screed it (see page 32) by drawing the two-by-four across it, and tamp again. Check with the level that the sand bed is even.

Lay the flagstones on the sand bed. To keep the sand level and undisturbed, avoid kneeling on it directly; place the sheet of polystyrene or plywood on the bed, and kneel on that. Settle each stone on the sand surface by tapping it gently with the mallet. If the stones vary in thickness, scoop out or fill in sand below each stone as necessary to keep the floor surface level.

When the stones are laid, prepare the gaps between them for planting. Using the trowel, remove as much sand as you can without eroding the sand under the stones, which must stay firmly in place to keep the floor level. Fill the gaps with the soil mix, to within ½ inch of the floor surface.

Plant the violets in the gaps between the stones. Space them 6 inches apart, or 3 inches if you want them to fill the gaps fast. Build the arbor over the patio, setting the corner posts outside the patio. Plant the rose and the porcelain vine on the north side of the arbor, so they'll grow over the arbor toward the sun.

OUTDOOR
SITTING AREAS

It's a pity to use a garden just for gardening. Only when idle do we notice the gray bloom on the blue mahonia berries, the bending trunk of the birch tree, the late-summer heat taking the strength out of the flower stems. It's in those moments, sitting on an upturned bucket or the curb of the lawn if necessary, that our hearts usually stir with pleasure.

Because sitting places are vital, do what landscape architects do: plan the patios in the garden before you consider the plants. A bench outside the door is a good start. If it's in view from the kitchen or the office, you'll see it become streaked with light when the sun breaks through after rain, and you'll be pulled outdoors to smell the warm steam rising off the leaves. If there's also a chair in a sheltered place in the vegetable garden, you may head out there and catch a few pristine puddles on the way.

Wherever you place your sitting areas, make them spacious. You'll want room to maneuver several pieces of furniture —logs, stools, chaises, whatever suits the character of the patio—from the shade into the sun; and room to stretch, walk around, and take in the view. There needn't be much of a natural view; it's enough to see how the land rises and falls around you and get a perspective on the plantings. Light, air, and shadows seem to flow more freely in open places, making the atmosphere calm and sweet.

SECRET SWING, VINEYARD VIEW

At the bottom of the garden—out beyond the pool, on past the flower beds, into the pergola, and then off at one end of it, as far from the house as you can go—hangs this swing with a view over a vineyard. Although the land is flat, you feel nicely perched here with your feet off the ground, a wisteria and your own grapevine making their way overhead, and tall sages and penstemons growing all about the sides.

From the fields, the pergola looks like more fence posts and more billowing vines against the blue sky. It would be hard to spot anyone swinging inside.

HOW TO DO IT ∽ This patio includes a foundation of 3 inches of crushed rock and a surface of 1 inch of decomposed granite (d.g.). In poorly draining soils, lay 6 inches of crushed rock. The patio is edged with wood two-by-fours.

The patio floor is the easy and inexpensive part of the project. The pergola is built of pressure-treated poles: the posts are 1 foot in diameter and sunk into concrete (before the patio is built); the beams are 10 inches in diameter, and the ceiling poles are 6 inches and 2 inches in diameter. The poles are heavy, so have a contractor build the pergola unless you are experienced in outdoor carpentry.

Before you start to lay the patio, check the sections on grading and drainage, pages 27 and 28–29.

Mark out the patio perimeter with the twine and stakes. This patio is 4 yards wide and 9 yards long, large enough for a 5-foot-wide table and four comfortable chairs in the middle of the pergola plus a side table and two more chairs at the opposite end. Set the twine ½ inch above the finished patio surface (see page 30) so you can use it to place the edging two-by-fours, which sit ½ inch higher than the d.g.

Excavate inside the patio perimeter to a depth of 4 inches. Firm the bottom of the excavation if you've disturbed the soil while digging.

Drive the stake one-by-twos into the sides of the excavation, outside the twine, at intervals of 8 feet. Position the edging two-by-fours so that they touch the twine, and nail them to the stakes, holding or wedging the stakes firmly upright during the hammering. Then hammer more stakes against the edging on the inside of the patio, to help prevent the edging from warping. Space them at intervals of 8 feet, between the outside stakes. Saw off any protruding stakes on the outside flush with the edging; on the inside, saw the stakes 1 inch below the edging, so they'll be hidden by the d.g.

Spread 3 inches of crushed rock into the bottom of the excavation, moisten it, and pack it down with the tamper.

Spread the d.g. 1 inch thick on the surface. Moisten it, and tamp the finished surface thoroughly.

Plant the Russian sage and the border penstemon 3 feet apart to make a bank around the swing. Plant vines in the garden to climb up the pergola poles: wisteria on both sides of the swing and grape vines on the other poles. Firm the soil outside against the patio edges.

Inexpensive in part (see text)
Easy in part (see text)
Location: Sun

Tools
Twine and stakes
Measuring tape
Straight-edged spade, for digging
Hammer
Saw
Shovel, for spreading materials
Hose
Hand-held tamper, or rented water-
    fillable roller or vibrator-plate
    compactor
Planting trowel

Ingredients
Pergola and swing (see text)
Redwood, heartwood cedar, or pressure-
    treated wood two-by-fours, for
    edging, length of patio perimeter
Stake one-by-twos, 18 inches long,
    1 stake per 4 feet of perimeter, and
    3-inch galvanized common nails
Crushed rock, ⅝- or ¾-inch, 3¼ cubic
    feet per square yard of patio
Decomposed granite (d.g.), ¼-inch
    minus, ¾ to 1 cubic foot per square
    yard of patio
Russian sage (*Perovskia* 'Blue Spire')
Border penstemon (*P. gloxinoides* 'Hunt-
    ington Pink')
2 wisteria vines
Grape vines (*Vitus*)

Maintenance
Water plants regularly until established,
    then less frequently
Remove Russian sage flowers when they
    die, and plant will bloom all summer
Rake patio regularly
Top up d.g. and tamp or roll every spring

FLAGSTONE CORNER
WITH BRICK SWIRL

This corner space in the shadow of an urban house has gained a vital, intimate life of its own. The flowing brick lines on the floor turn you off the main route around the house and through the arch to smell the 'Altissimo' rose climbing one of the columns. You're in a circle then of hypnotizing flowers and foliage in bright and dark hues of red combined with chartreuse. At your fingertips are fuzzy, matte-red kangaroo paw flowers and ribbed straps of variegated red-and-purple 'Tropicana' canna leaves. A seat invites you to stay for a while. If you do, you discover a restful view of islands of thyme growing through the brick-and-stone floor.

HOW TO DO IT ✐◦ This patio is laid on a foundation of 2 to

3 inches of gravel fines (½-inch minus), a suitable base if the ground drains well and doesn't freeze. In other situations, lay 4 to 8 inches of sharp-edged gravel beneath the fines, tamping it well. The brick portion of the patio is edged with recycled-plastic edging. The flagstone portion has no edging; see page 31 to decide whether you should install one.

Sketch your design on graph paper. Swirl the brick in a loop into the corner away from the house, to pull the eye out into the garden. Plan to place the arch so that it straddles the brick and flagstone, the brick sweeping between the columns. The columns in this garden are stucco-covered polystyrene, anchored in and filled with concrete; they are 6 feet tall and stand on 1-foot-high pedestals. The cross beam is wood, 6 inches by 10 inches; threaded rods anchor it to the tops of the columns. Have a contractor build and install the arch before you begin; or use a simple metal rose arch, and put it into position before laying the brick.

Before you start to lay the patio, check the sections on grading and drainage, pages 27 and 28–29.

Mark out the patio perimeter by making a circle at least 6 feet in radius (12 feet across): Hammer a nail into the top of each stake. Tie the twine to the nails. Hammer one of the stakes firmly into the ground at the center of the circle, and, keeping the twine taut, draw a circle in the dirt with the tip of the other stake. Using the same stake or a can of water-based marking paint, draw the perimeter of the paths adjoining the circle. Bleed the paths into the patio, to make a gradual transition with no sharp edges.

String twine across the patio area at the level of the finished patio surface (see page 30) so you can use it to place the brick and stone.

Excavate inside the patio and path perimeter to a depth of 5 inches. Firm the bottom of the excavation if you've disturbed the soil while digging.

Place the plastic edging on the sides of the patio where the brick will be. Install it so the top edge sits 1 inch below grade, so it won't be visible once the fines and bricks are in place. Secure the edging with the stakes.

Spread the gravel fines about 2½ inches thick, so the brick will sit slightly higher than the surrounding soil. Dampen the bed of fines, tamp it well, dampen again, and tamp again, until the bed is completely firm. In the brick section, screed it thoroughly (see page 32) by drawing the two-by-four across it, and tamp again. Check with the level that the bed is even.

Moderately expensive
Moderately difficult
Location: Sun or light shade

Tools
Graph paper and pencil
Hammer
Two stakes and nails
Piece of twine 6½ feet long, to mark out
    patio circle
Water-based marking paint (optional)
Twine and stakes, to mark finished surface
Measuring tape
Straight-edged spade, for digging
Shovel, for spreading fines
Hose
Hand-held tamper or rented water-
    fillable roller
Piece of straight two-by-four, for
    leveling fines
Level
Sheet of thick polystyrene or plywood,
    for kneeling on fines
Rubber mallet
Brick- and stone-cutting tools
    (see page 26)
Paper and scissors
Chalk, to trace cutting lines
Broom
Planting trowel

Ingredients
Arch (see text)
Recycled-plastic edging, two-by-four, with
    stakes, length of perimeter of brick
    section of patio
Gravel fines, ¼-inch minus,
    approx. 1 cubic yard for patio,
    plus extra for paths
Bricks, approx. 5 per square foot,
    "ironstone" or similar shade
Bluestone, for rest of patio, large pieces
    for better stability
Builder's sand, for filling joints between
    bricks
1 'Altissimo' climbing rose
Gray gravel, sharp-edged, ¼-inch, for
    filling joints between stones
Small plants such as creeping thyme
    (*Thymus praecox arcticus* 'Elfin'),
    for the paving gaps
Red and purple plants for the garden,
    such as *Cestrum fasciculatum*
    'Newellii', *Cotinus coggygria* 'Purple
    Robe', *Acer palmatum* 'Bloodgood',

(continued on next page)

Lay the bricks first. Start with the band of bricks that wraps around the flagstone edge of the patio, at the right edge of the photograph here. Lay the bricks in a running bond pattern, as shown. Place the bricks directly on top of the fines; don't wedge or push them in. Butt them against one another, not worrying about the inevitable tiny gaps between the bricks on the outside of the curve. To keep the fines bed level and undisturbed, avoid kneeling on it directly; place the piece of polystyrene or plywood on the bed, and kneel on that.

Settle each brick as you lay it by tapping it with the mallet. With the level, check that it's flush with the other bricks; if necessary, lift the brick and remove some fines or spread a little more underneath it.

Lay the rest of the bricks in the same manner. Cut bricks as necessary (see page 26) to make your pattern work. Plan to fill small spaces with plants.

Now lay the flagstones on the fines bed, arranging and rearranging them until you have a good fit with a minimum need for cutting. In small areas between the bands of brick, trace the outline of the area onto paper, cut around the outline, and place the cutout onto a piece of stone (or two stones well fitted) so you can draw around the cutout and cut the stone or stones to fit. Don't worry about small gaps between stones; you can fill those with plants. At the foot of one column, leave a space about 1 foot square to plant the rose.

Move the stones outside the fines bed in an orderly way so that you'll remember how they fit together. Spread more fines to raise the bed so that the flagstones will be flush with the bricks. Dampen the bed, tamp it, and check that it's level.

Cut the flagstones that don't fit well (see page 26). Place the flagstones back on the fines, settling each one with the rubber mallet and checking for level, just as you did with the bricks.

Sweep dry sand over the bricks and into the joints. Sprinkle the bricks with a hose to settle the sand, then top up the joints with a second sweep of sand, and sprinkle again.

Plant the rose and the small plants, first scooping out some of the fines with the trowel. Fill the joints between the stones and around the plants with gravel. Plant the garden plants, placing the chartreuse *Spiraea* in the corner to draw the eye.

Canna 'Tropicana', and *Abutilon megapotamicum*
2 or 3 chartreuse *Spiraea* 'Magic Carpet'

Maintenance
Water paving plants regularly
Water rose and garden plants regularly until established, then as recommended on labels
Refill gaps between bricks with sand periodically

SITTING ROOM
UNDER OAK BOUGHS

Very little disturbs the floor under the magnificent oaks in this garden. The leaves and acorns stay where they fall, and only an occasional fern interrupts the natural lay of the land and the waving line of old oak boughs above.

The woodland floor has been disturbed here to invite you into a dappled green room embraced by the tree's low limbs. The furniture was cut from local boulders; the concrete floor is recycled from a 1930s patio that wrapped around the house, down the slope.

HOW TO DO IT ᥥᥣᥤ This patio sits above grade on a shallow sand bed, to avoid disturbing the roots of the oak. If your soil freezes hard or drains poorly, the concrete pieces may tilt and have to be repositioned occasionally. The recycled concrete pieces are large (some are 3½ feet across).

Unless you can use boulders from your property, the boulder furniture may prove an expensive part of the project. To keep costs down, you might substitute simple flat-topped stones suitable to sit on or cut logs.

Before you start to build, check the sections on grading and drainage, pages 27 and 28–29.

Mark out the patio perimeter with the twine and stakes. Make it roughly circular, perhaps mimicking the shape of the tree canopy, and at least 12 feet across.

Excavate to a depth of 1 inch. Firm the bottom of the excavation.

Spread 1 inch of sand into the excavation, moisten it, and pack it down with the tamper.

Arrange the concrete pieces on the sand, leaving small gaps between them, so that rainwater will drain around each piece. Settle each piece as you lay it by tapping it with the mallet. Using the level, check that it's flush with neighboring pieces; if necessary, lift the piece and remove some sand or spread a little more underneath it.

Sweep soil from the excavation over the concrete pieces and into the joints. Sprinkle the patio with a hose to settle the soil, then top up the joints with a second sweep of soil, and sprinkle again.

If you don't have suitable boulders on your property, choose boulders from a stone yard for the furniture. Have the supplier cut out seats with slightly reclining backs from the larger boulders and make a flat table top on another. Place a couple of uncut boulders on the patio edge, for occasional seating.

Inexpensive in part (see text)
Easy
Location: Sun or shade

Tools
Twine and stakes
Measuring tape
Straight-edged spade, for digging
Shovel, for spreading sand
Hose
Hand-held tamper or rented water-
    fillable roller
Rubber mallet
Level
Broom

Ingredients
Builder's sand, 10 cubic feet
Concrete pieces, recycled, approx. 115
    square feet
Boulders, for furniture

Maintenance
Reposition concrete pieces occasionally,
    if necessary

BLUESTONE EDGED WITH GOLD

It's a steep descent from the house to this bluestone terrace carved out of the hillside, but all the way down you are lured by the glimpses of gold ahead. The entrance from the steps leads under the swaying branches of a green-gold robinia tree (R. pseudoacacia 'Frisia'). The foliage around the terrace is gold-green or splashed or edged with gold, and gold flowers bloom everywhere, including between the terrace stones.

Although elegant cut rectangles and squares of stone make up the terrace floor, the style is not stiff. Fragrant creeping thyme (Thymus citriodorus 'Aureus'), lady's mantle (Alchemilla mollis), and yellow violas have in-filtrated the geometry in places, as if seeds had blown in off the hillside and thrived in the rain dripping off the stones.

HOW TO DO IT ∽ This patio is laid on a foundation of 4 inches of crushed rock and 1 inch of sand. If your soil freezes hard or drains poorly, lay 6 to 8 inches of crushed rock. The patio has no edging; see page 31 to decide whether you should install one. Several spaces within the patio are left unpaved for planting.

Before you start to build, check the sections on grading and drainage, pages 27 and 28–29.

Draw the configuration of the stones on graph paper before you begin. Avoid a cluster of small slabs, and stagger the joints so that the edges of the stones make T intersections, rather than plus signs.

Mark out the patio perimeter with the twine and stakes. This patio is 15 feet long and 10 feet wide. Set the twine at the level of the finished patio surface (see page 30) so you can use it to place the stone.

Excavate below the twine to a depth of 5 inches plus the thickness of the stone. Firm the bottom of the excavation if you've disturbed the soil while digging.

Mix a slow-release fertilizer (optional) into the crushed rock for the patio base to help the patio plants grow. Spread 4 inches of crushed rock into the bottom of the excavation, moisten this layer, and pack it down with the tamper.

Mix more slow-release fertilizer (optional) into the sand. Spread 1 inch of sand over the crushed rock base. Dampen the sand and tamp it, then screed it (see page 32) by drawing the two-by-four across it, and tamp again. Check with the level that the sand bed is even.

Starting at a corner, lay the stone slabs. Butt the stones wherever you can, so there are no gaps between them. Gaps will develop inevitably around the smaller stones because of the way the stone is cut (most stone is trimmed short to allow for a mortar joint); try to avoid a sudden ½-inch gap; distribute the space between several stones if you can, or trim the long stone with a circular saw (see page 26). Leave a few squares or rectangles free of stone, so that you can plant in those spaces. To keep the sand bed level and undisturbed, avoid kneeling on it directly; place the sheet of polystyrene or plywood on the bed, and kneel on that. Settle each stone slab as you lay it on the sand by tapping it with the mallet. Using the level, check that it's flush with neighboring slabs; if necessary, lift the slab and remove some sand or add a little more underneath it.

Moderately expensive
Moderately easy
Location: Sun or light shade

Tools
Graph paper and pencil
Twine and stakes
Measuring tape
Straight-edged spade, for digging
Shovel, for mixing and spreading materials
Hose
Hand-held tamper, or rented water-
    fillable roller or vibrator-plate
    compactor
Piece of straight two-by-four, for leveling
    sand
Level
Circular saw, if necessary, for trimming
    stones
Sheet of thick polystyrene or plywood,
    for kneeling on sand
Rubber mallet
Broom
Planting trowel

Ingredients
Slow-release fertilizer (optional)
Crushed rock, ⅝-inch minus, 2 cubic
    yards
Builder's sand, ½ cubic yard, including
    sand for joints
Cut stone, 1½ to 2 inches thick, 150
    square feet
        three sizes of rectangles: 18 by 24
            inches (lots of these), 12 by 24
            inches, and 12 by 18 inches
        squares: 12 by 12 inches
Potting soil
Plants with yellow flowers, foliage, or var-
    iegations, such as yellow violas and
    ranunculus, *Carex elata* 'Bowles
    Golden', *Sedum alboroseum* 'Medio-
    Variegata', *Hedera* 'Buttercup', *Thymus
    citriodorus* 'Aureus', *Alchemilla mollis*

Maintenance
Water plants regularly
Refill joints with sand as necessary

To finish the patio, spread dry sand over the stones, and sweep it into the joints. Keep spreading and sweeping until the joints are full. Sprinkle the surface with a very fine spray from the hose to settle the sand in the joints. Top up the sand as necessary, and water again. Firm the soil outside against the patio edges.

Plant the empty spaces in the patio. Using the trowel, remove as much sand as you can without eroding the sand under the stones, which must stay firmly in place to keep the surface level. Fill the gaps with potting soil to within ½ inch of the surface. Plant into the soil.

PONDSIDE TERRACE

The wind stirs through the main garden up the slope. Down here on the quiet flagstone terrace by the kitchen, a turtle basks in the sun, and shoals of fish race their shadows across the bottom of the pond.

From the seats against the kitchen wall, the garden seems to come down the bank in one grand sweep of backlit aloes, grasses, and ground covers. The flagstone terrace doesn't quite hold it at bay; small creepers and succulents have set themselves up between the pieces of stone, and an aloe has found its way almost to the kitchen door.

HOW TO DO IT ⌀⊘

This flagstone terrace is laid on a foundation of 4 inches of gravel and 2 inches of sand. If your soil freezes hard or drains poorly, lay 6 to 8 inches of gravel. The terrace bleeds into the garden. It has no edging, but the stones are especially large to increase stability. See page 31 to decide whether you should install an edging.

The area where the terrace meets the pond needs special attention. Excavating close to a pond made with a flexible liner or preformed shell, or placing a boulder or paving stones there, can cause the bank supporting the liner to collapse or the shell to warp. The patio is the moderately easy and inexpensive part of the project. Have the pond built by an experienced pond installer. It's probably best to support the pond against a band of concrete or concrete blocks where it meets the terrace or to build a concrete pond. For safety's sake, the pond edge must be completely firm and sturdy enough to take the weight of the paving and a person standing on it.

Before you start, check the sections on grading and drainage, pages 27 and 28–29. Plan to pitch the terrace away from the pond, so the pond doesn't flood when it rains.

Mark out the perimeter of the terrace with the twine and stakes; let the edges follow the contours of the slope or the shape of existing flower beds. Set the twine at the level of the finished patio surface (see page 30) so you can use it to place the stone.

Excavate below the twine to a depth of 6 inches plus the thickness of the stone. Be especially careful not to disturb soil supporting the pond. Firm the bottom of the excavation.

Spread 4 inches of gravel into the excavation, moisten it, and pack it down with the tamper.

Before you lay the sand bed, install the boulder at the pond edge. Choose a boulder that's low and squarish or has a reclining shape; it will look most natural if you bury it to its widest point, but you don't want to dig a huge hole, so look for a boulder that's already widest at its base. Place the boulder on a promontory overlooking the pond if there is such a spot (a kidney-shaped pool works well for this). Rest the boulder's weight on solid ground, not on the pond rim, unless the rim is concrete and the pond installer is sure it will bear that much weight.

Lay the flagstones on the gravel. Choose the largest pieces for the pond

Moderately inexpensive in part (see text)
Moderately easy in part (see text)
Location: Sun or light shade

Tools
Twine and stakes
Measuring tape
Straight-edged spade, for digging
Shovel, for spreading materials
Hose
Hand-held tamper, or rented water-
    fillable roller or vibrator-plate
    compactor
Masonry saw, for cutting stone (see
    page 26)
Piece of straight two-by-four, for leveling
    sand
Level
Sheet of thick polystyrene or plywood,
    for kneeling on sand
Rubber mallet
Broom
Planting trowel

Ingredients
Gravel, sharp-edged, ⅝- or ¾-inch,
    3¼ cubic feet per square yard
    of terrace
Boulder; see text for suitable shape
Flagstones, large, 2 inches thick and
    preferably 3 by 3 feet, to cover terrace
Builder's sand, 1¾ cubic feet per square
    yard of terrace
Soil mix, for planting in gaps
Plants for the paving gaps: a few low-
    growing sturdy plants that are also
    growing in the neighboring garden,
    plus striking plants, such as aloes, for
    accents

Maintenance
Water plants regularly
Refill paving gaps with sand occasionally
Clean stone occasionally if light-colored
    and prone to staining

edge. Arrange them so the edges of the stones overhang the pond by 1 to 2 inches, to hide the pond edge. (If the stones are large, the weight is spread over a large area away from the pond rim. Large stones are also less likely to tilt when someone stands on the pond edge—an important safety concern.)

Rearrange the flagstones on the gravel until you have the best fit requiring the least amount of cutting. Leave gaps of 1 to 1½ inches between the stones for planting. The paving need not fit well around the boulder, because you will be planting in pockets of soil there. Trim the stones that need trimming (see page 26), and move all the stones outside the excavation in an orderly way so that you'll remember how they fit together.

Spread 2 inches of sand over the gravel base. Dampen the sand and tamp it, then screed it (see page 32) by drawing the two-by-four across it, and tamp again. Check with the level that the sand bed is even.

Lay the flagstones on the sand bed. To keep the sand level and undisturbed, avoid kneeling on it directly; place the sheet of polystyrene or plywood on the bed, and kneel on that. Settle each stone on the sand surface by tapping it gently with the mallet. If the stones vary in thickness, scoop out or fill in sand below each stone as necessary to keep the surface level.

To finish the patio, spread dry sand over the stones, and sweep it into the joints that you don't want to plant. Keep spreading and sweeping until the joints are full. Sprinkle the surface with a very fine spray from the hose to settle the sand in the joints. Top up the sand as necessary, and water again.

Prepare the remaining gaps for planting. Using the trowel, remove as much sand as you can without eroding the sand under the stones, which must stay firmly in place to keep the terrace level. Fill the gaps with soil mix, to within ½ inch of the surface. Plant in the gaps between the stones.

Firm the soil outside against the patio edges.

CONCRETE PAD IN THE WOODS

A concrete pad set down in the woods defies the tradition of establishing a transitional "garden" space between the house and the natural landscape. Here, modern architecture meets woodland squarely, and the contrast enhances each. Against the straight lines of the house, the lines of the tree trunks and the leafy canopies filigreed with sunlight seem particularly natural. And the patio feels particularly cozy, opening from the guest bedroom and the security of home.

Sitting here for a while, the tension in the contrast slips away, and harmony creeps in. The concrete is dappled like the lichen on the trees and contains the color of the striations in the native boulders. At your feet, the natural life of the woods continues uninterrupted.

HOW TO DO IT ⟊⟋ This concrete patio was poured onto a gravel foundation between wooden forms, which were removed when the concrete had set. The surface was colored to complement the house color and colors in the woods. The foundation and the forms are the easy parts of the project; unless you have experience working with concrete, have ready-mix concrete delivered and pumped to the patio site, and hire a contractor to pour and finish the concrete. Laying concrete is heavy work and costly to fix if it goes wrong.

The concrete rests on 4 inches of gravel. In a frost-free climate and freely draining soil, you could lay just 2 inches of gravel; if your soil freezes hard or drains poorly, lay 8 inches. (In very frosty areas, consider ordering concrete that includes an air-entraining agent.)

Before you start to build, check the sections on grading and drainage, pages 27 and 28–29. The patio should be pitched about ¼ inch per foot away from the house to allow water to run off.

Mark out the patio perimeter with the twine and stakes. Relate the size of it to the size of the indoor room. For example, extend it directly from the room walls and make it two-thirds as deep as it is wide. If the architecture contains square elements, such as square windows, perhaps make it square. Set the twine at the level of the finished patio surface (see page 30) so you can use it to place the forms.

Excavate below the twine to a depth of 8 inches. Excavate a few inches beyond the perimeter so you have room to place the wooden forms. Firm the bottom of the excavation if you've disturbed the soil while digging.

Spread 4 inches of gravel into the excavation, moisten it, and pack it down with the tamper. Check with the level that the gravel bed is even.

Make the forms for the concrete: Place the two-by-fours (be sure the lumber is rough; if you buy finished lumber, it will be only 3½ inches wide) around the edges of the excavation. The tops should touch the perimeter twine. If there is a gap between the forms and the gravel, spread more gravel and tamp it firmly, or the liquid concrete will slip under the forms.

Where two boards meet along a side, nail a 6-inch piece of one-by-four over the seam, on the outside. Brace the back of the lumber with your foot or a metal brace to keep it upright during nailing. Use double-headed nails, which will make the forms easier to dismantle later.

Moderately expensive
Easy in part (see text)
Location: Sun or shade

Tools
Twine and stakes
Measuring tape
Straight-edged spade, for digging
Shovel, for spreading gravel
Hose
Hand-held tamper or rented water-
    fillable roller
Level
Hammer
Brace (optional)
Saw, if necessary, to level protruding
    stakes
Paintbrush, for applying form-release
    agent
Wire cutter or heavy pliers, for cutting
    mesh (optional; see text)
Plastic sheet, to cover curing concrete

Ingredients
Gravel, sharp-edged, ⅝-inch minus,
    3 cubic feet per square yard of patio
For the forms:
    Two-by-four unfinished lumber, length
        of patio sides
    6-inch pieces of one-by-four, to use as
        splices (see text)
    Double-headed 3½-inch nails
    Stake two-by-twos, 2 feet long
Form-release agent
Wire reinforcing mesh with 6-inch grid,
    to almost cover patio area
Stones, to support mesh
Wire, to tie overlapping pieces of mesh
    (optional; see text)
Ready-mix concrete; give patio dimen-
    sions to supplier
Concrete color and sealant; discuss with
    contractor (see text)

Maintenance
Color may need reapplying periodically;
    discuss with contractor

Hammer stakes on the outside of the forms to secure them. Place a stake on each side of a corner and every 3 feet along the patio edges. Drive the stakes deep into the ground, and use at least two nails to nail them to the forms. The stakes must be strong and very secure or the concrete will push apart the forms. Pay particular attention to the corners and the places where the boards meet. If you can, hammer the stakes below the tops of the forms; otherwise, saw the tops off flush with the forms (the contractor will use the forms to level the concrete, so the stakes mustn't protrude above the forms).

With the paintbrush, grease the insides and tops of the forms with the form-release agent, so that you'll be able to slip the forms away from the concrete when it's set.

Lay the wire reinforcing mesh if you have the tools to cut it. Otherwise have the contractor do it. The wire should cover the patio area to within 2 inches of the forms and sit 2 inches above the gravel, so the mesh is roughly in the middle of the concrete when it's poured. Place stones on the gravel to support the mesh. Cut the mesh to fit. If you need to use more than one piece, overlap the edges by 6 inches, and tie the two layers together with wire.

The contractor needs to install an expansion strip between the patio and the house, so that the concrete doesn't crack as it expands and contracts with weather changes. As the concrete is poured, the contractor works it with a shovel or a hoe to remove air bubbles, especially from the corners, then screeds and floats (levels and smooths) the surface; brooms it to give it traction in wet weather; makes the jointing grooves, which control cracking as the concrete hardens; and runs the blade of a trowel and an edger around the patio so that the concrete doesn't chip when you remove the forms.

To make a colored finish, pigment is either added to the concrete mix or troweled or painted onto the finished surface. Discuss the color options with the contractor ahead of time; provide samples of the house paint or plant materials. (If you decide to stain the concrete surface, you can do this yourself; see page 48.) Make sure the finished surface will be rough enough to provide traction (a smooth surface will be dangerously slick underfoot after rain). The surface may also need sealing so the color doesn't fade.

Remove the forms three or four hours after the concrete is poured. Leave the concrete to cure for five days. Cover it with the plastic sheet so it doesn't dry out during hot weather.

ENTRANCE PATIOS

A welcoming space between the street and the front door is an important part of your property. It's here, before you've heard the bell, that your guests form a sense of your hospitality and let go of the stress of the long drive or a busy day. It's worth investing a lot of thought in how to make arriving at your home special.

Even if the distance between the street and the door is short, think of it as a journey, and try to extend the experience of the journey so that the arrival isn't abrupt. A gate, even if it's invitingly open, slows people down and marks beautifully the transition from public to private space. If it's fun or a piece of art, people may linger there for a moment, which is just what you want to achieve.

Extending the path inside the gate into a patio will slow people further. Even if they don't take a tour of the patio edges, they'll pause to gaze around the space before advancing on the front door. As long as you leave plenty of room for several people to arrive together, you can ornament the patio with sculpture, water bowls, bold plants (they should be good-looking all year round and easy to maintain), a rose arbor, a comfortable chair, a collection of fossils, or just about anything you please (except pieces that might snag clothes or trip someone or be easily knocked over). Alternatively, you might prefer a zenlike courtyard that offers little in the way of decoration but an exquisite feeling of shelter and calm.

RED AND GOLD WELCOME

Leaving the highway, you see a long, white modern house set on a small rise above the vineyards and embraced by a wooded canyon on three sides. The entrance is through a low tractor-red gate, a welcoming portal rather than a barrier, and then you step out of your car into the swaying shadows of trees.

Those are acts one and two of an artfully choreographed arrival. Act three starts with a breeze, translucent yellow leaves skittering about, and the music of water falling into a trough by the wall. Then the journey proceeds through this red gate into a courtyard around the front door.

The quiet inside is calming. A cart with metal books, wet with dew, stands against a gold wall (painted, on the suggestion of a feng shui expert, to draw richness around the house). Drifts of gold leaves rustle in the corners, and the poplar trees beyond the courtyard glitter against the sky. You won't mind waiting here for a minute, charmed by the succession of welcoming scenes since you left the highway, which now seems so far away.

HOW TO DO IT ❧ The cobbles in this courtyard were laid on a

bed of sand. The concrete path was poured onto a gravel foundation between wooden forms, which were removed when the concrete had set; brick red pigment was added to the concrete mix to make it look warmer, and the concrete was stamped into 2-foot squares after it was poured. The cobbles, the concrete foundation, and the forms are the moderately easy parts of the project; unless you have experience working with concrete, have ready-mix concrete delivered, and hire a contractor to pour and finish the path. Laying concrete is heavy work and costly to fix if it goes wrong.

The concrete rests on a foundation of 4 inches of gravel. In a frost-free climate and freely draining soil, you could lay just 2 inches of gravel; if your soil freezes hard or drains poorly, lay 8 inches. (In very frosty areas, consider ordering concrete that includes an air-entraining agent.)

To make a courtyard without incurring the expense of having walls built, plant a tall hedge around the finished floor (the walls here range from 6 to 10 feet, the lowest wall, the gold one, providing a view out to the trees). Alternatively, mark out the room with the trunks of trees, and let the leaf canopies provide the sense of shelter; arrange for a pool of light, no shade, at the front door.

Before you start to build the patio, check the sections on grading and drainage, pages 27 and 28–29. The concrete path should be pitched about 1½ inches across its width (or ¼ inch per foot along its length), away from the house to allow water to run off.

Mark out the path perimeter with the twine and stakes. Make it 6 feet wide. Set the twine at the level of the finished path surface (see page 30) so you can use it to place the forms.

Excavate below the twine to a depth of 8 inches. Excavate a few inches beyond the perimeter so you have room to place the wooden forms. Firm the bottom of the excavation if you've disturbed the soil while digging.

Lay the gravel foundation: Spread 2 inches of gravel into the excavation, moisten this layer, and pack it down with the tamper. Lay the next 2 inches in the same way. Check with the level that the gravel bed is even.

Make the forms for the concrete: Place the two-by-fours (be sure the lumber is rough; if you buy finished lumber, it will be only 3½ inches wide) around the edges of the excavation so the tops just touch the perimeter twine.

Moderately expensive
Moderately easy in part (see text)
Location: Sun or shade

Tools

Twine and stakes
Measuring tape
Straight-edged spade, for digging
Shovel, for spreading materials
Hose
Hand-held tamper or rented water-
    fillable roller
Level
Hammer
Brace (optional)
Saw, if necessary, to level protruding
    stakes
Paintbrush, for applying form-release
    agent
Plastic sheet, to cover curing concrete
Rubber mallet

Ingredients

Gravel, sharp-edged, ⅝-inch minus,
    3 cubic feet per square yard of path
For the forms:
    Two-by-four unfinished lumber, length
        of path perimeter
    6-inch pieces of one-by-four, to use as
        splices (see text)
    Double-headed 3 ½-inch nails
    Stake two-by-twos, 18 inches long
Form-release agent
Ready-mix concrete with 1 pound of
    brick-red pigment per cubic yard of
    concrete; give path dimensions to
    supplier
Builder's sand, 1 ½ to 1¾ cubic feet per
    square yard of cobbled area
Cobbles, in gray tones; give cobbled area
    dimensions to supplier

Maintenance

Sweep cobbles regularly

If there is a gap between the forms and the gravel, spread more gravel and tamp it firmly, or the liquid concrete will slip under the forms.

Where two boards meet along a side, nail a 6-inch piece of one-by-four over the seam, on the outside. Brace the back of the lumber with your foot or a metal brace to keep it upright during nailing. Use double-headed nails, which will make the forms easier to dismantle later.

Hammer stakes on the outside of the forms to secure them. Place a stake on each side of a corner and every 3 feet along the patio edges. Drive the stakes deep into the ground, and use at least two nails to nail them to the forms. The stakes must be strong and completely secure; concrete is heavy and will push apart flimsy forms. Pay particular attention to the corners and the places where the boards meet. If you can, hammer the stakes below the tops of the forms; otherwise, saw the tops off flush with the forms (the contractor will use the forms to level the concrete, so the stakes mustn't protrude above the forms).

With the paintbrush, grease the insides and tops of the forms with the form-release agent, so that you'll be able to slip the forms away from the concrete when it's set.

The contractor needs to install expansion strips between the path and the house, so that the concrete doesn't crack as it expands and contracts with weather changes. The pigment is added to the concrete during the mixing process. As the concrete is poured, the contractor works it with a shovel or a hoe to remove air bubbles, especially from the corners, then screeds and floats (levels and smooths) the surface, stamps it, and runs the blade of a trowel and an edger around the path so that the concrete doesn't chip when you remove the forms. Make sure the contractor roughly trowels the concrete into a travertine finish (or at least brooms it) to give it maximum traction; a smooth surface will be dangerously slick underfoot after rain.

Remove the forms three or four hours after the concrete is poured. Leave the concrete to cure for five days. Cover it with the plastic sheet so it doesn't dry out during hot weather.

Lay the cobbles once the path is in place. Mark out the courtyard perimeter, if it isn't already established, with the twine and stakes. This courtyard is approximately 20 by 25 feet; scale yours to the house architecture, making it generous so the space will feel gracious.

Excavate to a depth of 1 inch plus the approximate depth of the cobbles; with the sand bed in place, the cobbles will sit a little higher than the path. Firm the bottom of the excavation.

Spread 2 inches of sand into the excavation. Dampen the sand, and tamp it.

Arrange the cobbles on the sand. Settle each one as you lay it by tapping it with the mallet. Use the level to check that the cobbles are roughly flush with one another; if necessary, lift a cobble and remove some sand or spread a little more underneath it.

BLACK SLATE SEQUENCE

Although the front door isn't more than a few strides from the street, you don't arrive all at once. A carpet of black slate starts at the roadside. You cross that and the concrete sidewalk, and you arrive at this slate patio, where there's room to unload things from the car if you like. Up the steps between retaining walls, you reach another slate landing before the final step onto the porch.

The sequence of spaces and the changes in direction and level allow a gradual reorientation from the public realm—and the braced attitude most of us assume in public—to a more relaxed frame of mind, ready for friends. The rich planting helps change the pace too. At the entrance to the patio is a raised rock garden. Around the dark slate, flare mounds of golden yellow sweet flag.

HOW TO DO IT ⁓ This patio is laid on a foundation of 4 inches of crushed rock and 1 inch of sand. If your soil freezes hard or drains poorly, lay 6 to 8 inches of crushed rock. The joints between the stones are filled with sand. The patio has no edging; see page 31 to decide whether you should install one.

Before ordering the stone, discuss with the supplier how much the stones may vary in size. Some cut stone is not cut precisely and won't work well for this patio because you won't be able to get the lines straight. You can accommodate a slight variation in size if you identify the oversize and undersize stones and lay those at the first opportunity. If the variance is large, you'll need to trim the large stones and maybe discard the smallest.

Before you start to build, check the sections on grading and drainage, pages 27 and 28–29.

Mark out the patio perimeter with the twine and stakes. This patio is approximately 6 feet wide and 14 feet long (large enough to double as the legally required driveway). Set the twine at the level of the finished patio surface (see page 30) so you can use it to place the stone.

Excavate below the twine to a depth of 5 inches plus the thickness of the stone. Firm the bottom of the excavation if you've disturbed the soil while digging.

Spread 4 inches of crushed rock into the bottom of the excavation, moisten it, and pack it down with the tamper.

Spread 1 inch of sand over the crushed rock base. Dampen the sand and tamp it, then screed it (see page 32) by drawing the two-by-four across it, and tamp again. Check with the level that the sand bed is even.

To help lay the stones perfectly straight, string lines across the patio to mark the edge of each row of stones. Stake the lines outside the patio area. Slip the lines off the stakes to lay the stones, and then replace the lines to check that your rows are straight.

Starting at a corner, lay the stone slabs. Butt the stones, so there are no gaps between them, except to accommodate slightly undersized stones. To keep the sand bed level and undisturbed, avoid kneeling on it directly; place the sheet of polystyrene or plywood on the bed, and kneel on that. Settle each stone slab as you lay it by tapping it with the mallet. Using the level, check that

Moderately expensive
Moderately easy
Location: Sun or shade

Tools

Twine and stakes, for marking perimeter
    and rows of stone
Measuring tape
Straight-edged spade, for digging
Shovel, for spreading materials
Hose
Hand-held tamper, or rented water-
    fillable roller or vibrator-plate
    compactor
Piece of straight two-by-four, for
    leveling sand
Level
Sheet of thick polystyrene or plywood,
    for kneeling on sand
Rubber mallet
Broom

Ingredients

Crushed rock, ⅝-inch minus, 30 cubic
    feet, or 1⅛ cubic yards
Builder's sand, 9 cubic feet, including sand
    for joints
60 Pennsylvania black slate rectangles,
    12 by 18 inches, and at least 1½
    inches thick

Maintenance

Refill joints with sand as necessary

it's flush with neighboring slabs; if necessary, lift the slab and remove some sand or add more underneath it.

To finish the patio, spread dry sand over the stones, and sweep it into the joints. Keep spreading and sweeping until the joints are full. Sprinkle the surface with a very fine spray from the hose to settle the sand in the joints. Top up the sand as necessary, and water again. Firm the soil outside against the patio edges.

OUTDOOR ROOM FOR ONE

It was clever to divide a long wedge-shaped front yard into two spaces: one squarish garden at the thick end, where the main path could run fairly promptly from the sidewalk to the front door as in more regular yards; and the thin end of the wedge somewhat hidden, making a little room behind the street fence. It took the awkwardness out of the shape.

Interesting, though, the special qualities the tiny room assumed. It's separated from the house but not isolated from the larger neighborhood scene, as the backyard is. There's shelter and privacy here, sunshine glinting off the chartreuse and purple leaves, and fragrance from the roses, but also an enlivening sense of being still part of the world. An occasional bicycle hisses by on the tarmac; neighbors call out greetings to one another; children spill along the curb on their way to a game. It's a vibrant place between the private and public realms, a vantage point like a lace-curtained window seat.

HOW TO DO IT ⌒⌒ This Connecticut bluestone patio and its path are laid on a foundation of 2 inches of fines, a suitable base if the ground drains well and doesn't freeze. In other situations, lay 4 to 8 inches of sharp-edged gravel beneath the fines, tamping it well. There is no edging here; see page 31 to decide whether you should install one. Before you start to build, check the sections on grading and drainage, pages 27 and 28–29.

Plan the path so that it isn't immediately noticeable as you walk in from the sidewalk to the front door; you don't want to suggest an alternative to the main path. In this garden, the threshold of the path is hidden between a mound of lavender cotton *(Santolina chamaecyparissus)* and a pot of Mexican abelia *(A. floribunda),* and as you step from the sidewalk onto the main path you can't see the patio, because it's hidden behind the fence (which veers into the garden for a few feet) and a tall shrub *(Hypericum × inodirum* 'Albury Purple'). The path is 18 inches wide at the threshold; the patio swells out from the path to approximately 7 feet square.

Mark out the perimeter of the path and patio with water-based marking paint or twine and stakes. If you use marking paint, string twine across the patio area at the level of the finished patio surface (see page 30) so you can use it to place the stone. Excavate inside the perimeter to a depth of 2 inches plus the thickness of the stone. Firm the bottom of the excavation.

Place the flagstones inside the excavation. Rearrange the pieces until you have the best fit requiring the least amount of cutting. Leave gaps of 1 inch between the stones for planting. Trim the stones that need trimming (see page 26), and move all the stones outside the excavation in an orderly way so that you'll remember how they fit together.

Spread 2 inches of fines in the excavation, dampen them, and tamp them. Check with the level that the bed is even.

Lay the flagstones on the fines bed. To keep the fines level and undisturbed, avoid kneeling on them directly; place the sheet of polystyrene or plywood on the bed, and kneel on that. Settle each stone on the bed by tapping it gently with the mallet. If the stones vary in thickness, scoop out or fill in fines below each stone as necessary to keep the surface level.

Plant the creeping thyme between the stones, first scooping out some of the fines with the trowel. Space them 6 inches apart. Finish the patio by sweeping gravel into the joints and around the thyme plants. Firm the soil outside against the patio edges.

Moderately inexpensive
Easy
Location: Sun or light shade

Tools
Water-based marking paint (optional)
Twine and stakes
Measuring tape
Straight-edged spade, for digging
Stone-cutting tools (see page 26)
Shovel, for spreading fines
Hose
Hand-held tamper
Level
Sheet of thick polystyrene or plywood, for kneeling on fines
Rubber mallet
Planting trowel

Ingredients
Flagstone, large pieces, at least 18 and preferably 30 inches wide and 2 inches thick, approx. 50 square feet to cover patio, plus stones for path
Gravel fines, ¼-inch minus, approx. 9 cubic feet for the patio, plus 1½ cubic feet per square yard of path
Creeping thyme (Thymus praecox arcticus 'Elfin'), small plants in flats, for paving gaps
Gray gravel, sharp-edged, ¼-inch, to fill gaps between stones

Maintenance
Water thyme regularly until established and full, then less frequently
Clean stone occasionally if light-colored and prone to staining

STONE FLOOR,
STONE SCULPTURE

The small country road comes up from the Napa Valley through the vineyards stripped into the hills, past quiet land with lichened outcrops of rock and dusty fragrant scrub, to a high knoll, shady and mossy under oaks and dark-red-fruited madrones. A dirt road leads around the knoll, turns suddenly into the sun, and stops at this dramatic house terrace with a panoramic view.

No garden is in sight. Here is a celebration of the art of architecture and the beauty of native woodland and stone. The stucco house matches the color of the madrone fruit that drops onto the stone paths. The terrace wall and floor are natural compositions of ochre, rust, charcoal, honey, and mud, textured with shards of stone, crumbs of mortar, and soft rags of moss. Crowning the terrace are five natural stone spheres, part of a nest of round stones found in the ground in a neighboring valley.

HOW TO DO IT ∽ This patio is laid on a foundation of 2 to 3 inches of sand, a suitable base if the ground drains well. In other situations, lay 4 to 8 inches of gravel beneath the sand (see page 64). The stone is veneer stone; it has a fairly uniform thickness and a flattish, but rough, surface. (In cold-winter climates, to help prevent pools of ice from forming and making the entrance treacherous, do not lay stone with concave surfaces. Also make sure the patio pitches properly away from the house, so water drains off the patio.) The gaps between the stones are filled with earth-colored mortar.

Before you start to lay the patio, check the sections on grading and drainage, pages 27 and 28–29.

Mark out the patio perimeter with the twine and stakes. Scale it according to the architecture of the house and generously. This patio is approximately 25 feet square. Set the twine at the level of the finished patio surface (see page 30) so you can use it to place the stone. The patio here is laid as a platform a couple of inches higher than the entrance forecourt, a beautiful design detail, but be sure the surface of the patio sits at the required level below the house threshold.

To determine how deep an excavation to make, study your stone. The greater the variance in the thickness of the stones, the deeper your sand bed must be to accommodate it. If there's no more than a 2-inch difference in thicknesses, then a 2-inch sand bed is adequate. Excavate beneath the twine to the depth of the sand bed plus the average thickness of the stone. Firm the bottom of the excavation if you've disturbed the soil while digging.

Spread the sand into the excavation. Dampen and tamp it, then screed it (see page 32) by drawing the two-by-four across it, and tamp again.

Kneeling on the sheet of polystyrene or plywood, place the stones on top of the sand; don't wedge or push them in. With the level, check that each stone is roughly flush with the other stones; if necessary, lift the stone and remove some sand or spread more underneath it. Settle each stone as you lay it by tapping it with the mallet.

Aim to leave gaps of just 1 inch between the stones for the mortar. Although the patio is roughly finished by intention, the stones are very carefully laid. Arrange them so they fit well—for example, make the straight edges of adjoining stones parallel, and place a convex edge alongside a concave edge. In the inevitable large gap here and there, place a stone fragment or a small stone on edge.

Moderately expensive
Moderately difficult
Location: Sun or light shade

Tools

Twine and stakes
Measuring tape
Straight-edged spade, for digging
Shovel, for spreading sand and measuring mortar materials
Hose
Hand-held tamper, or rented water-fillable roller or vibrator-plate compactor
Piece of straight two-by-four, for leveling sand
Sheet of thick polystyrene or plywood, for kneeling on sand
Level
Rubber mallet
Rubber gloves
Mortar box
Hoe or mortar hoe
Mason's trowel
Piece of wood, for smoothing joints (optional)
Sponge

Ingredients

Builder's sand, approx. 1½ to 1¾ cubic feet per square yard of patio for a bed 2 inches deep
Veneer stone or fieldstone carefully selected for fairly uniform thickness and one flattish surface (see text); large variations in color and size are desirable
Mortar materials: portland cement, builder's sand, and fireclay (optional); or packaged Type M mortar with no lime
Mortar pigment to match stone color

Maintenance

Check mortar every year or so; patch if necessary

When the stones are in place, put on the rubber gloves, and prepare the mortar to go between them. In the mortar box, combine 1 shovelful of cement with 3 shovelfuls of sand, ½ shovelful of fireclay (optional; fireclay makes the mortar easier to work), and some mortar pigment. Measure the amounts fairly carefully; if you like, use a bucket instead of a shovel, but don't make too much mortar at once, because it will harden before you've used it. Mix the materials well with the hoe, form them into a pile, make a dent in the top, and add a little water. Mix thoroughly; then repeat, adding water until the mix is buttery and smooth (if it's too wet, it won't adhere as well to the stone).

Pack mortar between the stones with the mason's trowel. Smooth the joints roughly with the tip or edge of the trowel or a piece of wood; an uneven finish complements the rustic stone. Clean up any stray mortar splashes with the wet sponge as you work. To cure the mortar, keep the joints moist for several days by spraying them very lightly with the hose.

STOPPING PLACES

A garden that invites exploration, the most interesting kind of garden, needs a few small patios, or stopping places, along the paths. Arrange the patios so that people pause in a pool of sunshine against a bank where butterflies congregate, or in the melancholy darkness inside a tunnel of trees, or under an arch, fragrant with roses or tropical ginger, or any place with an invigorating view.

A stopping place can be a mere bulge in the path or a spacious terrace set at an intersection where several paths meet. Think about the microclimates in different parts of your garden in different seasons. Build a patio in a spot that catches the early morning sun and another to view the sun setting. Although we all love the sun, provide some places with shade, especially in hot climates. The contrast of light and dark areas in a garden is sensuous and dramatic and shouldn't be sacrificed even in a cool, cloudy region.

At Marjory Harris's garden in San Francisco (see page 94), designed by Harland Hand, the top of the garden is out of sight and remains so until you've climbed most of the hill. Steps go up in small flights through a miniaturized mountain landscape, over a waterfall, across slopes and meadows, and again and again open onto landings perched on the edge of the hillside. A bench, a table and chairs, a retaining wall, or a boulder provides a resting place and a different view across the garden and up or back down the trail. At the summit, the main patio has a view of the distant hills and still more places to explore—a secret patio with a cherub sitting at the edge of a pond, a raised patio under a wisteria arbor, and a quiet corner patio in the shelter of the sweet-smelling vines. When you are ready to descend, there's another path with little places all along it. You could spend hours in this garden, stopping at every bench and appreciating the rare plants blooming quietly in the warmth of the stones.

VEGETABLE GARDEN ESCAPE

It's a luxury to sometimes escape from a busy household and head off to the vegetable garden. Once there, you can decide whether to work or not. For a time, hoeing among the beans with the sun warming your back feels relaxing enough. The clouds are dispersing, and, looking over the fence, you can see the light moving across the landscape for miles.

As the sun warms the garden, the lounge prompts you to stretch out for a few minutes. Down at the level of the flowers and vegetables, the view changes scale—a sharply-fuzzy squash leaf, a silky-red bean flower, a colony of sunflower seedlings that have succeeded in the flagstone cracks. The breeze rustles the bean stalks against the poles, and the smell is of wilting weeds and ferny chamomile leaves.

HOW TO DO IT ∽ This patio is laid on a foundation of 2 inches of sand, a suitable base if the ground drains well and doesn't freeze. In other situations, lay 4 to 8 inches of crushed rock beneath the sand (see page 64). The patio has no edging; see page 31 to decide whether you should install one.

Before you start to build, check the sections on grading and drainage, pages 27 and 28–29.

Mark out the perimeter of the patio with the twine and stakes. Make it 9 feet square, which is large enough for a chaise and a side table. Set the twine at the level of the finished patio surface (see page 30) so you can use it to place the stone.

Excavate below the twine to a depth of 2 inches plus the thickness of the stone. Firm the bottom of the excavation.

Arrange the flagstones inside the excavation until you have the best fit requiring the least amount of cutting. Leave gaps of 1 to 2 inches between the stones for planting. Trim the stones that need trimming (see page 26), and move all the stones outside the excavation in an orderly way so that you'll remember how they fit together.

Mix a slow-release fertilizer (optional) into the sand for the patio base to help the patio plants grow. Spread 2 inches of sand in the excavation. Dampen the sand and tamp it, then screed it (see page 32) by drawing the two-by-four across it, and tamp again. Check with the level that the sand bed is even.

Lay the flagstones on the sand. To keep the sand bed level and undisturbed, avoid kneeling on it directly; place the sheet of polystyrene or plywood on the bed, and kneel on that. Settle each stone on the sand bed by tapping it gently with the mallet. If the stones vary in thickness, scoop out or fill in sand below each stone as necessary to keep the surface level.

Prepare the gaps for planting. Using the trowel, remove as much sand as you can without eroding the sand under the stones, which must stay firmly in place to keep the surface level. Fill the gaps with soil mix, to within ½ inch of the surface. Plant the chamomile in the gaps. Space them 6 to 12 inches apart, depending on how quickly you want them to fill. Firm the soil outside against the patio edges.

Moderately inexpensive
Easy
Location: Sun or light shade

Tools
Twine and stakes
Measuring tape
Straight-edged spade, for digging
Stone-cutting tools (see page 26)
Shovel, for mixing and spreading materials
Hose
Hand-held tamper or rented water-fillable roller
Piece of straight two-by-four, for leveling sand
Level
Sheet of thick polystyrene or plywood, for kneeling on sand
Rubber mallet
Planting trowel

Ingredients
Flagstone, large pieces, at least 18 and preferably 30 inches wide, and 2 inches thick, approx. 80 square feet to cover patio
Slow-release fertilizer (optional)
Builder's sand, approx. 15 cubic feet
Soil mix, for planting gaps
Chamomile (*Chamaemelum nobile*), small plants in flats, approx. 50 to 100

Maintenance
Water plants regularly until established and full, then less frequently
Shear plants occasionally to keep them neat
Clean stone occasionally if light-colored and prone to staining

BACKYARD BEACHCOMBING

At the foot of the garden stairs in the sun lies a pebble beach sparkling with pools of water and treasures tossed up by the tide. Explore it with the toe of your shoe and you may unearth a tiny Japanese landscape on a pottery shard or a pastille of green glass with a bright, liquid-looking center and edges dulled as if pounded in the waves. Looking close, you find a pebble that's a perfect pink pearl or so toffee-brown smooth you take it as a talisman and put it in your pocket.

A dry waterfall laden with more bounty pours through a gorge onto one side of the beach. On the other sits a Wish Fulfilling Stone, a heart-shaped rock with green-black swirls that shine when you trickle water from a nearby bowl over its face. There are fossils here, too, and stones carved with hiero-glyphics, and shells, of course. Before you leave, you could dip the treasures you've gathered into the water bowls to brighten them or rock to and fro on the bench, poring over your favorites one by one.

HOW TO DO IT ∽ This pebble beach patio is laid on a foundation of 2 inches of gravel fines (¼-inch minus), a suitable base if the ground drains well. In other situations, lay 4 to 8 inches of sharp-edged gravel beneath the fines, tamping it well. A layer of landscape cloth (optional) is laid beneath the fines to help suppress weeds. The patio is edged informally with interesting boulders and stones and water pots. The beach surface is a mix of many different sizes of Salmon Bay pebbles.

The inspiration for this beach was Glass Beach, in northern California, where an old landfill has been eroded by the Pacific Ocean, and glass and crockery pieces tumbled by the waves lie among car parts. Gather treasures for your beach from vacation spots, rock and gem stores, garage sales, and nature stores. To achieve a water-eroded finish to the pottery and glass, you'll need to tumble them. A noisy way of doing that is to put them in a cement mixer for a couple of days; or, to find a tumbler designed for the purpose, look in the Yellow Pages under Lapidary Equipment.

Before you start to build the patio, check the sections on grading and drainage, pages 27 and 28–29.

Mark out the patio perimeter with the twine and stakes. Make it at least 4 feet wide and let the edges flow into the garden in the shape of a bay if you like. To place a 5-foot bench on the patio (the bench swing shown here is over a bricked area that adjoins a brick path), make a space 8 feet long (leaving 1½ feet at either end of the bench) and 5 feet deep. Set the twine at the level of the finished patio surface (see page 30).

Excavate below the twine to a depth of 3 inches. Firm the bottom of the excavation if you've disturbed the soil while digging. Place a layer of landscape cloth in the excavation (optional).

Spread 2 inches of gravel fines into the bottom of the excavation, moisten them, and pack down the surface with the tamper.

Spread the pebbles 1 inch thick on the surface, moisten them, and tamp them into the gravel fines. Distribute the pieces of colored glass and pottery among the pebbles.

Place large stones and large water bowls on the patio edges. If you like, put colorful gravel or glass in the bottoms of the water bowls and floating plants on the surfaces, or plant papyrus and bog plants in pots, and immerse them in the water bowls. Make spills of colored glass pieces between the edging

Moderately expensive
Easy
Location: Sun or light shade

Tools
Tumbler, to smooth treasure pieces (see text)
Twine and stakes
Measuring tape
Straight-edged spade, for digging
Shovel, for spreading materials
Hose
Hand-held tamper or rented water-fillable roller

Ingredients
Treasure: lots of tumbled colored glass and pottery shards, interesting stones and boulders, fossils, carved stones, pretty gravels, anything treasure-like
Bench (optional)
Landscape cloth, area of patio (optional)
Gravel fines, ¼-inch minus, approx. 1¾ cubic feet per square yard of patio
Salmon Bay pebbles, wide variety of sizes, approx. 1 cubic foot per square yard of patio
Water containers: 2 or more large water bowls and water plants (optional)

Maintenance
Lightly brush large plant litter off pebbles regularly
Keep water containers filled to brim

stones. If you like, add small amounts of other decorative gravel, such as turquoise Indonesian pebbles around the foot of a blue or gray rock. Keep collecting so that you can replenish the decorative flotsam and jetsam after beachcombing children take home their favorite pieces.

CONCRETE LEDGE, MOUNTAIN MEADOW

Climbing up the garden, leaning a little into it occasionally to keep a sense of balance, you walk off the steps onto a large, comfortable ledge. There's a chance now to stand up tall and catch a long view back down and across the trail you just climbed—past the top of the waterfall, between rocky outcroppings, alongside miniature precipices, over gritty screes, each with its kaleidoscope of rock garden plants spilling from crevices or creeping in mats over stones.

Like every inch of the garden you've traversed so far, the ledge is thick with vegetation. Between the rocklike aged concrete slabs at your feet grow meadows of dwarf blue-eyed grass, pink thrift, alpine strawberries, erigeron, and a dozen or so other plants whose seeds have blown in from the slopes. A bench invites you to stay for a while before going on to the next resting place and a view of the garden summit.

HOW TO DO IT ∽ This ledge patio is made of concrete slabs,

4 inches thick, sculpted while wet directly on top of the soil, without a foundation. Like the garden steps, the slabs are edged with bricks recycled from an old garden patio. The tops of the slabs are smeared with dry cement to give them a rough, pocked, weather-worn appearance similar to stone. If your soil freezes or drains poorly, excavate the patio area and lay 8 inches of sharp-edged gravel below the slabs. In very cold climates, handmade concrete may not be sufficiently durable; talk to a supplier, and consider ordering a batch of ready-mixed concrete that contains an air-entraining agent. Be warned that making concrete is heavy work, so take it slowly.

Mark out the patio perimeter with the twine and stakes. Make it roughly 6 feet wide and 15 feet long, adding room for the bench at one end, if you like. Draw out the slab shapes in the dirt with a stick, some chalk, or marking paint. The sizes vary; no two are the same. At the top of the steps on the left side of the patio, the slab is 54 inches long by 19 inches wide. At the top of the far steps, the slab is 44 inches long by 36 inches wide. Between them are two slabs: one 37 inches by 28 inches, the other 28 inches square. Behind this row, from right to left, are slabs 48 by 28 inches, 36 by 27 inches, 36 by 30 inches, 18 by 12 inches, 24 by 24 inches, and behind the latter two a slab 44 by 30 inches. Nothing is regular in the layout; the patio edges jig to and fro, as if following the contours of the hillside. The gaps between the slabs are 6 inches wide; because no adjoining slabs are the same size, the gaps do not align. In one place, next to the smallest slab, there's a large plant pocket measuring 36 by 14 inches. Arrange your slabs as you wish; just be sure to make most of them very generous in scale.

Before you start making the first slab on top of the ground, excavate to a depth of 3 inches on the edge of the slab where the bricks will sit, so you can give the bricks a concrete foundation. Slope the inside edge of the excavation like a bowl, and extend it beyond the width of the bricks, so the concrete beneath the bricks will be well connected to the rest of the slab.

Put on the rubber gloves to keep the cement off your skin. In the bucket or wheelbarrow, thoroughly combine the dry materials for the first concrete slab (start with a small one, such as the one 24 inches square). Measure the materials—1 part cement, 4 parts sand, 1 part pea gravel—in level shovelfuls. Once the mix is uniform, add water, gradually, turning and mixing with the shovel

Moderately inexpensive
Moderately easy
Location: Sun

Tools
Twine and stakes
Measuring tape
Stick, chalk, or marking paint, to draw
    shapes in dirt
Straight-edged spade, for digging
Rubber gloves
Bucket or wheelbarrow, for mixing
    concrete
Shovel, for measuring, mixing, and moving
    concrete
Hoe (optional)
Hose or watering can
Builder's trowel, rectangular, for sculpting
Brick-cutting tools (see page 26)
Plastic sheet or wet cloths, if weather
    turns wet or hot
Planting trowel

Ingredients
For a stone 24 inches square, approx. 1¾
    cubic feet of concrete, composed of
    1 part cement
    4 parts builder's sand
    1 part pea gravel
(For the entire patio, approx. 2½ to 2¾
    cubic yards of concrete)
Bricks, approx. 50
Potting soil
Diminutive plants, such as thrift (*Armeria*,
    dwarf species), blue-eyed grass
    (*Sisyrinchium bellum*, dwarf forms),
    muscari, dwarf erigeron, alpine
    or red-flowering strawberry
    (*Fragaria* spp.)

Maintenance
Water most plants regularly until
    established, then less frequently
Thin plants so that no one species
    becomes invasive
Let slabs accumulate moss, algae,
    and cracks

or hoe as you go, until it's "a little wetter than sand for sand castles," according to Harland Hand, the landscape architect of this garden. The mix should be firm enough to hold its shape on the shovel. If it becomes too wet, leave it for a while.

Shovel the concrete onto the marked area. With the trowel, first fill the excavated area and then spread a layer 1½ inches thick across the slab. Place bricks along one edge, leaving roughly 1-inch gaps between the bricks and filling them with concrete. (To cut a brick, see page 26.) Spread the rest of the slab so that the surface is flush with the tops of the bricks, tamping and smoothing the concrete with the trowel. Using your gloved hands, taper the three edges of the slab that have no bricks, so that, once the gaps between slabs are filled with soil, the slab will seem to be rising from bedrock. Give the slabs a hand-made quality; the surfaces of Harland's slabs undulate a little, and the edges are soft, not precise.

Before the concrete sets, sprinkle a handful or two of dry cement onto the surface of each slab where it would get the most wear. Once it has absorbed some moisture from the wet slab, trowel it into the surface until it's shiny.

Make the other slabs, leaving planting gaps of at least 6 inches between them. Wash the concrete off the tools before it dries.

Wait five days for the concrete to cure. Cover the slabs with the plastic sheet if it starts to rain. Cover them with the wet cloths if the weather turns hot and dry.

Fill the gaps between and around the slabs with the potting soil. Plant diminutive low-growing rock garden plants, especially creeping types, and miniature bulbs.

SHADOW PLAY
AND DECORATIVE EXCESS

Like a maze, this garden was designed to confuse and evoke tension and delight. The layout is simple seen from above: a small rectangular lot bordered by a cypress hedge and thirteen tiled planters set out in straight lines on a large central patio. Walking in the garden, though, you are purposefully misled by the visual cues. The north-south axes seem to be the main ones, but they don't lead to the garden's main destination. That lies at the end of a diagonal axis that takes you back on yourself once or twice.

The paving is no help; at moments it has a directional pattern, but then that pattern dissolves and you're stranded looking down at "L8R" ("later"), dizzy both from being thwarted and from the fragrance of the old roses in every planter, the dazzling checkerboard patterns, the crowd of "excess babies," and the hypnotic, intellectual writings about the meanings of shadows.

This is all as it should be. You're free now of your normal expectations of a garden walk. You can lose yourself in reverie.

HOW TO DO IT 〰 This patio floor is composed of new and sec-

ondhand brick and inexpensive concrete pavers in various colors and shapes. It can be laid on a foundation of 1 to 2 inches of sand if your ground drains well and doesn't freeze. In other situations, lay 4 to 8 inches of gravel beneath the sand (see page 64). The pavers are laid tightly; some of them have an easy interlocking pattern, but you'll need to cut the units to make other patterns fit (see page 26). The patio can be edged in various ways: with an invisible plastic edging designed for bricks (see page 45), or a wood edging (see page 39), or a recycled-plastic edging (see page 59).

In this garden, designer Frances Butler has incorporated a story of the meaning of shadows—that they are laden with associations of death, power, and fear and also of safety, delight, and play. You might choose a subject that interests you and present it in visual imagery and in text written on the vari-ous garden surfaces. The garden destination should reveal the subject in some way; in this garden the destination is a mortuary shrine. Then plan to deco-rate the garden excessively, to overload the senses. Use diverse flower colors and fragrances, repeated dizzying patterns, and challenging sculptures or objects. Don't hesitate to take the design into the sky; Frances has shadow-casting letters mounted on overhead trellises and long checkerboard wands leaning against the garden walls.

This garden has built-in high maintenance: the roses must be fertilized, deadheaded, and pruned, the planter tiles washed, the signs dusted, and the patio swept. Frances welcomes this work, because the repetitive small tasks induce reverie, which she finds is an entry into creativity.

Draw the patio design on paper. Establish a simple grid for the planters, and decide on the garden destination. Place it in a corner of the garden, at the end of a diagonal, but block that diagonal with a planting bed or a trellis, so that you have to weave onto another diagonal and cross back to find it.

Roughly design the paving. To stop yourself from relating the paving pat-tern to spaces between the planters, remove the planter positions from your paper and design the paving as sometimes flowing freely, sometimes struc-tured, constantly changing shapes within the patio boundaries. Then place the planters onto it, rotating them at different angles to increase disorienta-tion, and adapt the paving so that it looks directional in a couple of places—for example, to welcome people onto the patio from a side gate or the foot of the stairs that lead out from the house, make a directional pattern there.

Inexpensive
Moderately easy
Location: Sun

Tools
Graph paper and pencil
Twine and stakes
Measuring tape
Straight-edged spade, for digging
Shovel, for spreading sand
Hose
Hand-held tamper or rented water-
    fillable roller
Level
Hammer
Piece of straight two-by-four, for
    leveling sand
Sheet of thick polystyrene or plywood,
    for kneeling on sand
Rubber mallet
Brick- and concrete-cutting tools (see
    page 26)
Broom

Ingredients
Builder's sand, approx. 1 1/2 cubic feet per
    square yard of patio, including sand
    for joints
Edging (for options, see text)
Miscellaneous bricks and concrete pavers
    for patio surface
Planters and decorative elements (see
    text)

Maintenance
Refill paving joints with sand as necessary

Before you start to build, check the sections on grading and drainage, pages 27 and 28–29.

Mark out the patio perimeter with the twine and stakes. Set the twine at the level of the finished patio surface (see page 30) so you can use it to place the paving.

Excavate inside the perimeter to a depth of 1 inch plus the thickness of the bricks, or the thickest pavers if they are thicker than the bricks. Firm the bottom of the excavation.

Spread 1 inch of sand into the excavation. Dampen the sand, and tamp it.

Place the edging along the sides of the excavation. Secure it firmly.

Starting at a corner of the patio, screed an area of sand thoroughly (see page 32) by drawing the two-by-four across it, and tamp it again. Check with the level that the sand bed is even.

Lay the brick section of the pattern first. Place the bricks directly on top of the sand; don't wedge or push them in. To keep the sand bed level and undisturbed, avoid kneeling on it directly; place the sheet of polystyrene or plywood on the bed, and kneel on that. Settle each brick on top of the sand by tapping it with the mallet. With the level, check that it's flush with the other bricks; if necessary, lift it and remove some sand or spread a little more underneath it.

To lay the concrete pavers, you first need to top up the sand bed so the pavers sit flush with the bricks. Be sure to tamp and screed the sand several times before laying each section, so the base is always completely firm. Cut bricks or pavers so that they fit tightly. Use the level to keep the patio even.

To finish the patio, spread dry sand over the surface, and sweep it into the joints. Keep spreading and sweeping until the joints are full. Sprinkle the surface with a very fine spray from the hose to settle the sand in the joints. Top up the sand as necessary, and water again. Firm the soil outside against the patio edging. Arrange the planters and other decorative elements.

HIDEAWAYS

A garden is remembered as magical if it has a place so hidden that the owner leads you there or you perhaps come upon it, almost embarrassed by your keen sense of exploration. Suddenly, in your imagination the garden divides into two realms, the areas open to everyone and the secret place. And like a shrine, it's what's most hidden that registers most deeply.

Once you set your heart on making a hideaway, several places may come to mind. The space must be small. If it's far from the house, it will likely be quieter, which is another essential quality, and it will require a longer journey and therefore seem more special. Look along the garden boundaries; take advantage of a natural dip in the ground or a few square yards behind a thicket of bamboo or on the far side of a hedge or tree. Maybe there's room to carve an alcove into the flower beds or among shrubs off to one side of the lawn. Consider any dead spaces such as narrow passageways on the sides of the house or places lost in the undergrowth at the top of the hill.

To ensure that your hideaway feels sequestered, make access to it a little difficult. Instead of a wide path or the sight of a bench, clear signals calling people toward a destination, take the path through many turns, and make the cues on this journey subtle. You might even drop all cues along a stretch of the path, to let the sense of order and civilization fall away, and then present the tip of an umbrella just visible through the trees. When the umbrella has been out of sight for some time, you might again affirm that this is the right track by placing an obelisk in a flower bed nearby.

If you are lucky enough to have a natural feature on your property that inspires awe, such as a stream or a view of a valley or a gothic house or magnificent boulders like those on the hillside of the Santa Barbara garden shown on page 112, place your hideaway there. Otherwise, place something in your hideaway that is special to you, something that is whimsical or symbolic or that refreshes the spirit and that people will feel privileged to come upon.

BORROWED URBAN VIEW

A neighbor's beautiful old house looms over the garden wall. It's on a hilltop, its romantic faded pink facade, iron grille balconies, and stone obelisks silhouetted against the sky. The little garden here in its shadow borrows it as a backdrop and view.

A pink-throated bower vine roams over the aged pink stucco wall. Oriental fountain grasses with pink-blush seedheads whisper through the other garden plantings, including purply pink penstemons and pink-flowering and purple-leafed coral bells. Canadian Sunset flagstone, streaked naturally with pink, fords the brick pathway through the patio. Between the patio stones lie pretty pink and buff Salmon Bay pebbles.

HOW TO DO IT ◇◇

This patio is laid on a foundation of 2 to 3 inches of gravel fines (¼-inch minus), a suitable base if the ground drains well and doesn't freeze. In other situations, lay 4 to 8 inches of sharp-edged gravel beneath the fines, tamping it well. The patio has no edging; see page 31 to decide whether you should install one.

Sketch your design on graph paper. Swirl the brick path from the patio entrance through the patio toward a focal point, such as the birdbath between the columns here, in the foreground of the borrowed view.

Before you start to lay the patio, check the sections on grading and drainage, pages 27 and 28–29.

Mark out the patio perimeter with the twine and stakes or the marking paint. If you use marking paint, string twine across the patio area at the level of the finished patio surface (see page 30) so you can use it to place the brick and stone. Make the patio at least 6 feet wide and as long as you like.

Excavate inside the patio perimeter to a depth of 5 inches. Firm the bottom of the excavation if you've disturbed the soil while digging.

Spread the gravel fines about 2½ inches thick; place a brick on the fines and check that the top of the brick just touches the twine. Dampen the bed of fines, and tamp it well. Along the brick path section, dampen it again, screed it thoroughly (see page 32) by drawing the two-by-four across it, and tamp again. Check with the level that the brick section of the bed is even.

Make the brick path first. Lay the bricks eight courses wide in a running bond pattern, as shown. Place the bricks directly on top of the fines; don't wedge or push them in. Butt them against one another, not worrying about the inevitable tiny gaps between them on the outsides of the curves. To keep the fines bed level and undisturbed, avoid kneeling on it directly; place the sheet of polystyrene or plywood on the fines, and kneel on that.

Settle each brick as you lay it by tapping it with the mallet. With the level, check that it's flush with the other bricks; if necessary, lift the brick and scoop out some fines or spread more underneath it.

Now lay out the streaked pink flagstone on either side of a curve in the path. Arrange the pieces so they seem to flow in a band across the brick path. Let the edges intrude well into the path (you'll remove and cut bricks to make room for them). Rearrange the stones until you have the best fit requiring the least amount of cutting. In tricky areas, trace the outline of the area to be

Moderately expensive
Moderately difficult
Location: Sun or light shade

Tools

Graph paper and pencil
Twine and stakes
Water-based marking paint (optional)
Measuring tape
Straight-edged spade, for digging
Shovel, for spreading fines
Hose
Hand-held tamper or rented water-fillable roller
Piece of straight two-by-four, for leveling fines
Level
Sheet of thick polystyrene or plywood, for kneeling on fines
Rubber mallet
Paper and scissors
Stone- and brick-cutting tools (see page 26)
Chalk, to trace cutting lines
Broom
Planting trowel

Ingredients

Gravel fines, ¼-inch minus, approx. 2½ cubic feet per square yard of patio
Bricks, approx. 5 per square foot of brick path
8 pieces of Canadian Sunset flagstone, or similar pink-streaked stone, for inset into path
Buff flagstone for rest of patio, large pieces for better stability
Builder's sand, small bag, for filling joints between bricks
Salmon Bay pebbles, for filling gaps between flagstones
Creeping thyme (*Thymus praecox arcticus* 'Elfin')
Black mondo grass (*Ophiopogon planiscapus* 'Nigrescens')
Pink and purple plants for garden, such as pink bower vine (*Pandorea jasminoides* 'Rosea'), coral bells (*Heuchera micrantha* 'Palace Purple'), and *Penstemon gloxinoides* 'Sour Grapes'
Oriental fountain grasses (*Pennisetum orientale* 'Pink Blush')

filled onto paper, cut around the outline, and place the cutout onto a piece of stone (or two stones well fitted), so you can draw around the cutout and cut the stone to fit. Don't worry about small gaps between stones; you can fill those with the Salmon Bay pebbles or plants.

Cut the flagstones as necessary (see page 26). Trace onto the bricks the outline of the stones that intrude into the path. Lift the bricks, and cut them along the trace line (see page 26).

Lay out the rest of the flagstones. Leave gaps of ½ to 1 inch between the stones for the pebbles. Trim the stones that need trimming, and move all the stones outside the excavation in an orderly way so that you'll remember how they fit together.

Spread more fines across the patio to raise the bed, so that the flagstones will be flush with the bricks. Dampen the bed, tamp it, and check that it's level.

Place the flagstones back on the fines, settling each one with the rubber mallet and checking that they are level, just as you did with the bricks.

Sweep dry sand over the brick path and into the joints. Sprinkle the bricks with a hose to settle the sand, then top up the joints with a second sweep of sand, and sprinkle again. The firmly settled sand locks the bricks in place, so be sure to fill the joints well.

Sweep the pebbles over the flagstones and into the gaps between them. Settle them by sprinkling them with the hose. Sweep more pebbles until the gaps are full.

Plant the largest gaps with thyme or black mondo grass, first scooping out the pebbles and some of the fines with the trowel.

Firm the soil outside against the patio edges. Plant pink and purple plants and fountain grasses around the patio.

Maintenance
Water plants regularly
Refill gaps with sand and pebbles
  periodically

CITY MANDALA

In 1991, the year of the American bombing of Baghdad, Emil Miland and Fredric Sonenberg created this garden refuge out of a slab of concrete as a personal commitment to peace. The mandala design—concentric circles within a square—they copied from a Tibetan wall hanging. They borrowed too the idea of a group of skulls, a memento mori, at the heart of the mandala, placing them in a circular pond.

What strikes you as you enter their city garden is not death but the beauty of life and living things. Walking out of the kitchen and down the stairs, you pass a blessing hand of Buddha and descend through the tops of a Brazilian butterfly tree (Bauhinia), a jacaranda, and a persimmon. Tropical-looking Fuchsia boliviana *and Chinese bellflower* (Abutilon) *have threaded themselves through the tree branches, creating tall, flowering, green walls around the patio below. There, painted wooden tropical fish swim in the angel's trumpet* (Brugmansia versicolor 'Charles Grimaldi'), *and goldfish glide among the skulls.*

HOW TO DO IT ✂ This patio is made from an existing concrete patio slab cut into pieces. It is laid on 1 inch of sand, a suitable base if the ground drains well and doesn't freeze. In other situations, lay 4 to 8 inches of sharp-edged gravel beneath the sand (see page 64). The gaps between the concrete pieces are filled with a light-colored gravel. There is no edging, so the concrete pieces may eventually tilt a little in places if the sand base or soil moves.

The raised concrete pond in the center of the garden was made by pouring concrete into a mold (the fountain pump sits at the bottom of the pond; the electrical cable goes out through the pond wall and under the patio floor). While the concrete was still soft, Indonesian turquoise pebbles were studded into the outer surface. Instead of the pond, you might place a very large raised water bowl or a series of water bowls at the center of the garden.

You can break up a concrete slab yourself with a masonry saw or jackhammer rented from a tool supply company, but it is slow, hard, dusty work. To make this an easy project, call in a contractor to cut the concrete; check the Yellow Pages under Concrete Breaking, Cutting, and Sawing. Before the cutting starts, decide on the size of the pieces, and mark a few on the concrete slab. Avoid small pieces; although they are easier to lift and move, many small pieces make a patio look fussy. If you like, make distinctively octagonal or square pieces.

Before you start to build, check the sections on grading and drainage, pages 27 and 28–29.

Mark out the patio perimeter by making a circle 10 feet in radius (20 feet across): Hammer a nail into the top of each stake. Tie the twine to the nails. Hammer one of the stakes firmly into the ground at the center of the patio, and keeping the twine taut, draw a circle in the dirt with the tip of the other stake.

Excavate inside the perimeter to a depth of 1 inch plus the thickness of the concrete. Firm the bottom of the excavation.

Place the concrete pieces inside the excavation. Rearrange them until you have a good fit. Leave gaps of 1 to 2 inches between the pieces for the gravel. Move the concrete pieces outside the excavation in an orderly way so that you'll remember how they fit together.

Spread 1 inch of sand in the excavation. Dampen the sand and tamp it, then

Inexpensive
Easy in part (see text)
Location: Sun or light shade

Tools
Rented masonry saw or jackhammer
   (optional; see text)
Chalk, for marking cuts in concrete
Hammer
Two stakes and nails
Piece of twine 10½ feet long
Measuring tape
Straight-edged spade, for digging
Shovel, for spreading materials
Hose
Hand-held tamper, or rented water-
   fillable roller or vibrator-plate
   compactor
Piece of straight two-by-four, for
   leveling sand
Level
Sheet of thick polystyrene or plywood,
   for kneeling on sand
Rubber mallet

Ingredients
Recycled concrete, large pieces, approx.
   315 square feet to cover patio
Builder's sand, 1 cubic yard
Gravel, light-colored, decorative, to fill
   gaps between concrete pieces
Raised pond or water bowl for patio
   center
Water-loving plants, for some gaps
   in concrete near water feature
   (optional)

Maintenance
Refill gaps with gravel periodically

screed it (see page 32) by drawing the two-by-four across it, and tamp again. Check with the level that the sand bed is even.

Lay the concrete pieces on the sand bed. To keep the sand level and undisturbed, avoid kneeling on it directly; place the sheet of polystyrene or plywood on the bed, and kneel on that. Settle each concrete piece on the sand surface by tapping it gently with the mallet.

To finish the patio, tip gravel into the gaps between the concrete pieces. Sprinkle the gaps with spray from the hose to settle the gravel. Top up the gravel to within ½ inch of the surface. If you like, once you've placed a water feature at the patio center, plant lush water-loving plants into some of the gaps around it.

Firm the soil outside against the patio edges.

FOLLOW THE BRICK LINES

The path at the end of the main patio contains a solicitation. It's subtle: the boulder catches the eye, and at first glance the brick pattern in the paving seems simply decorative. But look twice, and the pattern seems to beckon. On a nudge from some part of the brain that has picked up the cue, your feet will lead you there eventually, and you'll come upon another patio, more quiet and hidden than the first.

Only the window over the kitchen sink looks onto the patio in this area of the garden. There's no sign of it from any other part of the house or anywhere in the yard. Some form of attractive invitation had to be extended so people would gather there.

HOW TO DO IT ⌐∾

This patio and path are laid on a foundation of 4 inches of crushed rock and 1 inch of sand. If your soil freezes hard or drains poorly, lay 6 to 8 inches of crushed rock. The joints between the stones are filled with sand. The patio has no edging; see page 31 to decide whether you should install one.

Before ordering the stone, discuss with the supplier how much the stones may vary in size. Some cut stone is not cut precisely and won't work well for this patio because you won't be able to get the lines straight. A slight variation in size can be accommodated if you identify the oversize and undersize stones and lay those at the first opportunity. If the variance is large, you'll need to trim the large stones and maybe discard the smallest.

To make the brick lines in the path, rent a tool to cut the brick and stone (see page 26). The brick pattern in the patio requires no cutting.

Before you start to build, check the sections on grading and drainage, pages 27 and 28–29.

Mark out the patio and path perimeter with the twine and stakes. The path is 6 feet wide as it approaches the corner, narrows to 4½ feet on the turn, and then swells to 7½ feet. The patio is 9 feet wide and 11 feet long. Set the twine at the level of the finished patio surface (see page 30) so you can use it to place the stone.

Excavate below the twine to a depth of 5 inches plus the thickness of the stone. Firm the bottom of the excavation if you've disturbed the soil while digging.

Spread 4 inches of crushed rock into the bottom of the excavation, moisten it, and pack it down with the tamper.

Spread 1 inch of sand over the crushed rock base. Dampen the sand and tamp it, then screed it thoroughly (see page 32) by drawing the two-by-four across it, and tamp again. Check with the level that the sand bed is even.

To help lay the stone perfectly straight, string lines across the patio to mark the edge of each row of stone. Stake the lines outside the patio area. Slip the twine off the stakes to lay the stone, and then replace the lines to check that your rows are straight.

Starting at a corner, lay the stone in the path area. Butt the stones, so there are no gaps between them, except to accommodate slightly undersized stones. To keep the sand bed level and undisturbed, avoid kneeling on it directly;

Moderately expensive
Moderately difficult
Location: Sun or shade

Tools

Brick- and stone-cutting tools (see page 26)
Twine and stakes, for marking perimeter and rows of stone
Measuring tape
Straight-edged spade, for digging
Shovel, for spreading materials
Hose
Hand-held tamper, or rented water-fillable roller or vibrator-plate compactor
Piece of straight two-by-four, for leveling sand
Level
Sheet of thick polystyrene or plywood, for kneeling on sand and stone
Rubber mallet
Mason's chalk or crayon
Broom
Planting trowel

Ingredients

Crushed rock, ⅝-inch minus
    for path: 3¼ cubic feet per square yard
    for patio: 1⅓ cubic yards
Builder's sand, including sand for joints
    for path: ¾ to 1 cubic foot per square yard
    for patio: 9 cubic feet
Pennsylvania black slate, rectangles 12 by 18 inches, at least 1½ inches thick
    for path: 6 per square yard
    for patio: 60
Bricks, to complement color of stone
    for path: 35
    for patio: 100
Soil mixed with crushed rock, for plant pockets
6 small sedum plants

Maintenance

Water sedum regularly until established, then less frequently
Refill joints with sand as necessary

place the sheet of polystyrene or plywood on the bed, and kneel on that. Settle each stone slab as you lay it by tapping it with the mallet. Using the level, check that it's flush with neighboring slabs; if necessary, lift the slab and remove some sand or spread a little more underneath it.

When the path is laid, lay the brick on top of the stone in two diagonal lines, as shown in the photograph. Place the sheet of polystyrene or plywood on the stone, and walk or kneel on that. Chalk or crayon the outline of the brick lines on the stone. Put the bricks to one side. Cut the stones that need cutting (see page 26). Lay the bricks, in the same manner as the stones, excavating some of the sand so the bricks sit flush with the stones.

Lay the stones and bricks in the patio area. Stagger the lines of brick as shown. Leave gaps for plants where the bricks don't fit exactly into the spaces between the stones.

To finish the patio, spread dry sand over the stones and bricks, and sweep it into the joints. Keep spreading and sweeping until the joints are full. Sprinkle the surface with a very fine spray from the hose to settle the sand in the joints. Top up the sand as necessary, and water again.

Plant the paving gaps. Using the trowel, remove as much sand as you can without eroding the sand under the stones or bricks, which must stay firmly in place to keep the surface level. Fill the gaps with soil-rock mix, to within ½ inch of the surface. Plant the sedum into it.

Firm the soil outside against the patio edges.

ROCK SANCTUARY

Coming in between the pride-of-Madeira bushes, you step into a pool of sunshine sheltered from the wind blowing off the Pacific Ocean. Blue jays yak in the native oak and bay trees. Bees drone through the pride-of-Madeira flowers on the banks. The scaly, mineral-marked faces of the monumental rocks are warm to the touch.

Dropping into a seat or walking to the patio edge to take in the view, you find that time slips away, and the silence is almost holy. Even before the patio was built to mark this as a site of pilgrimage, people probably made their way up the hill from the house through the undergrowth to find refuge here.

HOW TO DO IT ∽

This patio includes a foundation of 4 inches of crushed rock and a surface of 2 inches of decomposed granite (d.g.). In a dry climate and freely draining soil, you could lay just 2 inches of crushed rock; in poorly draining soils, lay 6 inches. The patio is bordered with native sandstone at the entrance and on the side with the view; the stone is laid on 1 inch of sand. This patio has no edging; see page 31 to decide whether you should install one.

Site the patio alongside an existing boulder or any treasured natural feature, such as an old tree or flowing water. If you like, make a flagstone path to the patio: Excavate it and lay the foundation in the same way as you do for the patio; finish it by brushing d.g. between the stones or brushing a dry mix of 1 part cement and 3 parts sand between them, and watering it with a very gentle spray.

Before you start to build the patio, check the sections on grading and drainage, pages 27 and 28–29.

Mark out the patio perimeter by making a circle 9 feet in radius (18 feet across): Hammer a nail into the top of each stake. Tie the twine to the nails. Hammer one of the stakes firmly into the ground at the center of the circle, and keeping the twine taut, draw a circle in the dirt with the tip of the other stake.

String twine across the patio area at the level of the finished patio surface (see page 30) so you can use it to place the stone and d.g.

Excavate inside the patio perimeter to a depth of 6 inches. Firm the bottom of the excavation if you've disturbed the soil while digging.

Spread 4 inches of crushed rock into the bottom of the circle, moisten it, and pack it down with the tamper.

Lay the sandstone or flagstone border on top of the crushed rock. Rearrange the pieces until you have the best fit requiring the least amount of cutting. Trim the stones that need trimming (see page 26), and move all the stones outside the excavation in an orderly way so that you'll remember how they fit together.

Spread 1 inch of sand onto the crushed rock where the stone border will be. Dampen the sand and tamp it, then screed it (see page 32) by drawing the two-by-four across it, and tamp again. Check with the level that the sand bed is even.

Inexpensive
Easy
Location: Sun or light shade

Tools

Hammer
Two stakes and nails
Piece of twine 9½ feet long
Twine and stakes, to mark finished surface
Straight-edged spade, for digging
Shovel, for spreading materials
Hose
Hand-held tamper, or rented water-fillable roller or vibrator-plate compactor
Circular saw for trimming stone (see page 26)
Piece of straight two-by-four, for leveling sand
Level
Sheet of thick polystyrene or plywood, for kneeling on sand
Rubber mallet
Planting trowel

Ingredients

Crushed rock, ⅝-inch minus, 3¼ cubic yards
Sandstone or flagstone, large pieces at least 1½ inches thick, to border part of perimeter
Builder's sand, ¾ cubic foot per 1 square yard of sandstone or flagstone border
Decomposed granite (d.g.), ¼-inch minus, 1½ cubic yards
Small stones, to fill gaps between sandstones or flagstones
Bench
7 pride-of-Madeira (*Echium fastuosum*), or, in cold climates, butterfly bush (*Buddleia davidii*)

Maintenance

Water plants regularly until established, then less frequently
Cut or shear flower spikes when they fade
Rake patio regularly
Top up and tamp d.g. every spring

Lay the sandstone or flagstone on the sand bed. The stone should sit a little higher than the d.g. (so the d.g. won't wash over it when it rains). To keep the sand bed level and undisturbed, avoid kneeling on it directly; place the sheet of polystyrene or plywood on the bed, and kneel on that. Settle each stone on the sand by tapping it gently with the mallet. With the level, check that it's flush with the other stones; if necessary, lift the stone and remove some sand or spread a little more underneath it.

Tamp the crushed rock foundation if you've disturbed it while laying the stone, and check that it's level.

Spread 2 inches of d.g. onto the crushed rock, packing it tightly around the stone border. Fill any gaps between the sandstones or flagstones with small stones so that the d.g. cannot wash away. Dampen the d.g., and tamp the finished surface thoroughly. Firm the soil outside against the patio edges.

Place the bench in the shelter of the boulders. Plant one pride-of-Madeira on each side of the entrance to the patio and the others around the patio and behind the bench to make shelter. Leave part of the boundary open toward a pleasant view. Space the plants 4 feet apart; plant them 2 feet from the patio edge.

CALCULATING QUANTITIES
OF MATERIALS

All the recipes in this book contain lists of ingredients that include the amounts of each material you'll need to build the patio. If you decide to make a deeper patio base or a larger or smaller patio, use the following information to calculate the amounts you'll need.

Loose materials, such as crushed rock, gravel, and sand, are sold by the cubic foot or cubic yard. Multiply the width of the patio, in feet, by the length of the patio, in feet, and the depth of the material, also in feet; then add 10 percent for safety's sake. For example, for a patio 8 feet wide and 10 feet long that requires a 2-inch layer of sand, you'd need 15 cubic feet of sand ($8 \times 10 \times 0.17$, plus 10 percent). That's more than half a cubic yard—divide cubic feet by 27 to convert to cubic yards.

Bricks are sold individually. To allow for some breakage and a small store for repairs, calculate on the basis of 5 bricks per square foot of patio if the bricks are standard size. Measure your patio by multiplying the width, in feet, by the length, in feet. For a patio 8 feet wide and 10 feet long, order 400 bricks ($8 \times 10 \times 5$).

Concrete and mortar are purchased by the cubic foot or cubic yard. Multiply the width of the concrete slab, in feet, by the length of the slab, in feet, by the thickness of the slab, in feet; then add 10 percent for error. Divide by 27 to convert cubic feet to cubic yards.

If you're buying bags of ready-mix concrete or mortar, read the back of the bag to see how many bags you'll need. If you're mixing the ingredients from scratch, calculate the amounts of the individual materials as follows: add the part numbers together (for example, 1 part cement, 2 parts sand, 3 parts gravel = 6 parts); divide the total quantity of concrete, say 50 cubic feet, by that number ($50 \div 6 = 8.33$); then multiply each part by that number—8.33 cubic feet of cement, 16.67 cubic feet of sand, 25 cubic feet of gravel. Add 10 percent to each order.

Cut stone is sold by the square foot. Multiply the width of your patio, in feet, by the length of your patio, in feet. A patio 9 feet wide and 14 feet long will require 126 square feet of stone. Decide on the size of the stones. If they'll be 18 inches square, you'll need 56 stones ($1.5 \times 1.5 = 2.25$; $126 \div 2.25 = 56$). If you're laying stones of several sizes, draw the pattern on graph paper, and count the number of each size. Be aware that cut stone has a nominal size and an actual size. The nominal size is, say, 18 inches by 24 inches; the actual size is perhaps 17¾ inches by 23¾ inches, cut short to allow for a ½-inch mortar or sand joint. If you are butting different sizes of cut stone, occasional gaps between the small stones are inevitable (see page 64).

Irregular pieces of flagstone, fieldstone, and pebbles may be sold by weight or by the pallet load. Multiply the width of your patio, in feet, by the length, in feet, and give that number to the supplier. He or she will help you estimate how many stones to start off with.

GLOSSARY

Benderboard: a wood edging in different thicknesses that is somewhat flexible, inexpensive, and easy to install but not long-lasting unless it's redwood, heart-wood cedar, or pressure-treated wood

Brick set: a chisel-like tool with a 4-inch edge for cutting brick

Builder's sand: clean sand sold at building supply yards and home improvement centers for construction; not beach sand

Construction chalk: white powder sprinkled on the ground to mark out a path perimeter; twine and stakes are better for straight lines

Crushed rock, crushed stone: mechanically crushed, sharp-edged stone; packs well and makes an excellent path foundation

Cut stone: stone snap-cut or sawed into squares and rectangles; sawed stone has a sharper, cleaner edge than snap-cut stone

Decomposed granite, d.g.: naturally broken stone particles ranging in size from small gravel to sand

Fieldstone: natural stone from a hillside or field, unfinished

Fines, finings: dust from mechanical crushing of rock; creates a sandy texture in gravel and helps it pack down well

⅝-inch minus: stone crushed mechanically to angular pieces ⅝ inch and smaller, with the crushing dust, or fines, added in; packs well and is comfortable underfoot

Flagstone: stone split into random paving slabs with irregular edges or into regular cut stone squares and rectangles; soft flagstone may stain easily and crack

Float: a flat piece of wood or steel with a handle, used to smooth out the surface of wet concrete

Foundation materials: layers of crushed, sharp-edged rock and sand that pack down well and provide a firm surface for brick, flagstone, concrete pavers, or decorative gravels

Freely draining soil: soil through which water passes quickly after heavy rains; for a drainage test, see page 28

Gazebo: a garden building with a roof and open sides

Gravel: small stones crushed mechanically (with angular edges) or collected from rivers or other natural deposits (with round edges); see also Crushed rock, Pea gravel

Landscape fabric: a synthetic porous cloth that helps suppress weeds, available in various widths and lengths

Landscape tie: a pressure-treated length of four-by-six or six-by-six lumber; easier to work with and better for the garden than used railroad ties, which are often warped and saturated with creosote

Mortar: a mix of cement, sand, either lime or fireclay, and water for joints between bricks or pavers; sweep off any spills as you work, and remove stains with a 10 percent solution of muriatic acid

¼-inch minus: see ⅝-inch minus

Pea gravel, peastone: round stones suitable only for a patio surface; they slide and roll and are therefore unsuitable for patio foundations

Pergola: a series of columns or posts on either side of a path with wires or cross beams overhead, often covered with vines

Poorly draining soil: soil through which water does not pass quickly after heavy rain; for a drainage test, see page 28

Rootball: the ball of roots and the soil that clings to them when a plant is lifted from the ground or a pot

Screed: to smooth and level sand or wet concrete by pulling a length of wood back and forth over it

Tamp: to compact until firm, using a hand-held heavy tamping plate on a pole, a water-fillable drum roller, or a vibrator-plate compactor

Veneer stone: split stone normally used to face a wall

BIBLIOGRAPHY

The following books have inspired and informed my writing on patios:

Alexander, Christopher, Sara Ishikawa, and Murray Silverstein. *A Pattern Language.* New York: Oxford University Press, 1977.

Brookes, John. *John Brookes' Garden Design Workbook.* London: Dorling Kindersley, 1994.

Butler, Frances. *Colored Reading: The Graphic Art of Frances Butler.* Berkeley, Calif.: Lancaster-Miller, 1979 (out of print).

Church, Thomas D., Grace Hall, and Michael Laurie. *Gardens Are for People.* Berkeley and Los Angeles: University of California Press, 1995.

Crowe, Sylvia. *Garden Design.* Wappingers Falls, N.Y.: Antique Collectors' Club, 1994.

Eck, Joe. *Elements of Garden Design.* New York: Henry Holt & Co., 1995.

Hicks, David. *Garden Design.* London: Routledge & Kegan Paul, 1982.

Keen, Mary. *Decorate Your Garden: Affordable Ideas and Ornaments for Small Gardens.* London: Conran Octopus, 1993.

Page, Russell. *The Education of a Gardener.* New York: HarperCollins Publishers, 1994.

Sunset National Garden Book. Menlo Park, Calif.: Sunset Books, 1997.

Walls, Walks, and Patios. Upper Saddle River, N.J.: Creative Homeowner Press, 1997.

Wilkinson, Elizabeth, and Marjorie Henderson, eds. *Decorating Eden: A Comprehensive Sourcebook of Classic Garden Details.* San Francisco: Chronicle Books, 1992.

Yoshikawa, Isao. *Elements of Japanese Gardens.* Tokyo: Graphic-sha Publishing, 1990.

ACKNOWLEDGMENTS

I'm very grateful to the many landscape architects and garden designers who shared their enthusiasms about patios with me, especially Jack Chandler, Rich Haag, Marcia Donahue, Suzanne Porter, Isabelle Greene, Susan Van Atta, Dan Borroff, Sharon Osmond, and David Yakish.

Saxon and I are also greatly indebted to all those who opened their gardens to us for this book. Thank you for your generosity and hospitality—we were inspired by it.

Thanks to Chronicle Books for putting the book together beautifully, in particular to our editor, Leslie Jonath, managing editor Dean E. Burrell Jr., copy editor and dear friend Zipporah Collins, and designers David Bullen and Julia Flagg.

And many thanks to my family and friends, especially Margarita Kloss, Carol Henderson, Barbara Berry, and Tom Hassett.

GARDEN CREDITS

Gardens and garden owners are listed in roman type; the landscape architect or designer in italics.
Jack Chandler, *Jack Chandler & Associates:* pages 1, 74, 76, 77. Vinton S. Sommerville, *Richard Haag, FASLA, RAAR:* pages 2, 3, 17, 20, 34 bottom, 41, 43. *Marcia Donahue:* pages 4, 91, 93. *Suzanne Porter:* pages 6, 7, 19, 28, 81, 82, 103, 105. Jane Stutfield, *Suzanne Porter:* pages 9, 33, 58, 60. *Isabelle Greene, Santa Barbara:* pages 8, 10, 11, 14 top, 31, 61, 62, 86. *Van Atta Associates:* pages 12 top, 13 top and bottom, 26. *Sharon Osmond:* pages 12 bottom, 18 bottom. *Heide Stolpestad Baldwin:* page 14 bottom. Ron and Eva Sher, *Richard Haag, FASLA, RAAR:* pages 15, 27. *Sydney Baumgartner, Santa Barbara:* pages 16 top, 51, 53. Susan Pollock, Seattle, *Dan Borroff Landscape:* pages 16 bottom, 63, 65. Sanford Winery, *Van Atta Associates:* pages 18 top, 54. Scurlock residence, *Nancy Hammer Landscape Design:* pages 21, 38, 40. *Jack Chandler & Associates:* pages 23, 69, 71, 83, 85. Tom Nelson, *Jack Chandler & Associates:* pages 24, 56. *Dan Borroff Landscape:* pages 29, 44, 46, 78, 80, 89, 109, 111. *David Yakish, gardenmakers:* pages 30, 32, 47, 49 (sculpture by Marcia Donahue), 72. Gary and Karen Kledzik, *Van Atta Associates:* pages 25, 112, 114. David Gemes: page 34 top. Stephen Greenholz, *gardenmakers:* pages 35, 36. Kent Gullickson and Joe Frankenfield: pages 66, 68, 100, 102. Marjory Harris, *Harland Hand:* pages 94, 96. *Frances Butler:* pages 97, 98, 99. Emil Miland and Fredric Sonenberg: pages 106, 108.

INDEX